A Treasury
of
Inspirational Illustrations

Earl C. Willer

BAKER BOOK HOUSE
Grand Rapids, Michigan

ISBN: 0-8010-9557-3

Printed in the United States of America

Contents

He Signed an Unwritten Letter

Frequently individuals in public office receive unsigned letters, commonly called "anonymous" or "crank letters." For the most part these letters, unsigned and filled with hatred and/or "well-meaning" advice, are products of warped and small minds. When D. L. Moody was conducting evangelistic meetings across the country, he too often faced hecklers who were in rather violent disagreement with his beliefs and tenets, and who often wrote such letters.

In the final service of one campaign, an usher handed the famed evangelist a note as he entered the auditorium. Supposing it to be an announcement, Moody quieted the large audience and prepared to read the notice. He opened it to find the single word: "Fool!" But the colorful preacher was equal to the occasion. He said, "This is most unusual. I have been handed a message which consists of but one word—the word 'fool.' I repeat, this is most unusual. I have often heard of those who have written letters and forgotten to sign their names—but this is the first time I have ever heard of anyone who signed his name and forgot to write the letter!" And taking advantage of the situation, Moody promptly changed his sermon to the text: "The fool says in his heart, 'There is no God' " (Ps. 14:1).

"The fool says . . . 'There is no God.' " It should go without saying that the more man learns of the universe, the more he becomes astounded with the inroads that science has made, the more he learns of the magnitude of nature, the less he dare claim that the world in which he lives has come into being by "chance" or by "happenstance." The astronauts who landed on the moon, the first humans so to do, were enthralled by the "desolate magnificence" of what they saw, and even though there was no deep theological implication in their statements they certainly were impressed with the immensity of a partial glimpse of the galaxy of stars and planets viewed from the long distance away from the place called home—the earth.

How one can live day by day without giving one single thought to that Power or Force that is responsible for life and living is incomprehensible to one who even momentarily wonders about a "creation." He must cry out with the psalmist when he says, "What is man that thou art mindful of him, and the son of man that thou dost care for him?" (8:4). In comparison to all that is visible the individual is so insignificant. But he is considered important and worthwhile through the activity of Jesus Christ, the God-Man, who came into the world to save him. Only the fool says, "There is no God."

Crackers-and-Cheese Christians

A number of years ago, a Scotchman arrived in Liverpool, England, where he was to set sail on a ship bound for America. He looked carefully at the few shillings that made up his total earthly capital, and decided that he would economize on food during the trip in order to have more money on hand when he landed at New York. He went to a small store and laid in a supply of crackers and cheese to get him through the days at sea. As the voyage progressed the sea air made him very hungry. To make matters worse the dampness in the air made his crackers soft and his cheese hard. He was almost desperate with hunger. To cap the climax he caught the fragrant whiff of food on a tray a steward was carrying to another passenger. The hungry man made up his mind that he would have one good, square meal, even though it might take several of his shillings. He awaited the return of the steward and asked him how much it would cost to go to the dining room and get a dinner. The steward asked the Scotchman if he had a ticket for the steamship passage. The man showed his ticket, and the steward told him that all meals were included in the price of the ticket. The poor man could have saved the money he spent on crackers and cheese; he could have gone to the dining room and eaten as much as he liked every mealtime.

How like the "Cheese-and-crackers" man are the children of the heavenly Father. Saved by the grace of God, and having the promise of fellowship with Him immediately, there are those who, refusing to appropriate for themselves the joy of divine reconciliation, go about with the soggy crackers and rancid cheese of life. Paul reminded the Romans (8:32 KJV) that "He that spared not his own Son, but delivered him up for us all, how shall he not with him freely give us all things?" Everything that is necessary for a full and complete life, with meaning and destiny, is found in Jesus Christ, who has paid for the passage on the boat of life. His death and resurrection is the ticket that entitles the individual to the finest, most comfortable arrangements with "all meals provided."

Hungry Without Reason

A few days after the Civil War had been officially ended, a man was riding along a road in West Virginia. Suddenly a soldier, clad in a dirty and tattered Confederate uniform, sprang out of a thicket, seized the horse's bridle, and with twitching face demanded, "Give me bread! Give me bread! I don't want to hurt you, but give me bread—I'm starving." The man on horseback replied, "Then why don't you go to the village and get food?" "I don't dare—they will shoot me," was the soldier's answer. "What for?" inquired the man; "tell me your trouble."

The Confederate soldier related that he had deserted his company several weeks before. Upon approaching the Union pickets, however, he had been informed that no fugitives from Lee's army were to be taken in. What was he to do? If he returned to his company, he would be shot as a deserter. In desperation he had taken to the woods and lived there on roots and berries until starvation had driven him to the point of madness. The man on horseback listened, and then exclaimed: "Don't you know the war is over? Lincoln has pardoned the whole Confederate army. You can have all the food you want." Taking a newspaper from his pocket, he showed the account of Lee's surrender and the president's proclamation of amnesty. With a shout of joy, the soldier dropped the bridle and ran for the village. That starving deserter did not know that the bread for which he hungered had been available to him for some time and could have been had for the asking. In his ignorance he had been self-deprived.

There are numerous people in the world today who are starved and starving for "food" for the soul. The so-called "soul food" found in the "in" spots will never bring contentment for the inner man who hungers and thirsts after righteousness anymore than will the elegant foods found on elaborate menus of fashionable restaurants. Jesus said, "I am the bread of life; he who comes to me shall not hunger, and he who believes in me shall never thirst" (John 6:35). To a far greater degree than any human being could

9

find possible, the living God has granted total "amnesty" to those who come to Him in the name of Jesus Christ, His Son, the world's Savior. There is no reason for anyone to hunger. "The Bread of Life" offers Himself fully and freely to anyone who will partake.

Atonement

You Can't Do It by Yourself

Years ago, a family lived in California. The father had been born in Virginia, the mother, in New York. The Virginia grandfather had never seen his daughter-in-law or his grandchildren, so he determined to visit the West to see his family. His coming caused great joy and great preparation. The house was painted; the curtains were cleaned; everything was pointed toward Grandfather's visit. Grandfather will be here in two months; in a week; in three days; tomorrow. Then he arrived. He was a handsome old gentleman of the South, with a white beard like General Lee's, and a twinkle in his blue eyes. The small grandson was impressed with his grandfather and took a special interest in Gramp's slippers. The slippers had soft leather tops and loops in front and in back by which they were pulled on the foot. One day the five-year-old put his feet, shoes and all, into the slippers, and reached down and put his fingers in the loops. The grandfather said, "Pull hard, my boy, and see if you can lift yourself off the ground." The boy tugged and tugged, and the old man said, "Well, that's too bad. You'll have to eat some more oatmeal, and then we will try again tomorrow."

The little boy had stopped eating in the midst of his breakfast —there were more important things than food! The parents urged him to eat, and then Grandfather took charge. He reminded the boy that the slippers were waiting, and that there would be another trial when breakfast was over. If the movement of the spoon stopped for too long a period, the old man would wink at the boy, make a gesture toward his room where the slippers were, and the boy would speedily go to work on his oatmeal. When breakfast was concluded, the pair, old and young, went solemnly into the bedroom where another trial was made. The little boy pulled and tugged, but he could not lift himself off the ground. The old man said, "Well, we didn't make it this morning, but we'll try again tomorrow."

So often this is the case of the natural man. He feels that he can lift himself by his own bootstraps, if he will only "eat" enough of the world's advice. But he cannot lift himself to higher levels. Only if the Lord, the Christ, the Savior, brings strength to him, can he hope to rise to the level that is God pleasing. It is God that lifts, as the psalmist says, "He brought me up also out of an horrible pit, out of the miry clay, and set my feet upon a rock, and established my goings" (40:2 KJV). You can't do it yourself!

Bible

Explaining the Ocean

It seems that a man once went to Atlantic City on a business trip and checked into a fine new hotel with an enjoyable view of the Atlantic Ocean with its ever-changing moods and majesty. A friend, who had never been to the coast, asked him to describe the beauties and wonders of the Atlantic in a letter, and he wrote as follows:

"I have a beautiful room, and a picture window gives me a sweeping view of the ocean. The window is 12 feet 2 inches long and 4 feet 8 inches high. It is divided into three sections. I have had a scraping of the glass analyzed and can tell you the chemical formula of it. An expert from one of the glass companies told me all about the glass. Am enclosing a history of the invention and development of glass. The steel frames are painted black. The analysis of both steel and paint have been made and are enclosed in a second and third study affixed to this letter. The putty used to keep the glass in the frames has also been analyzed and a long addenda on the chemical composition of it is also attached. The window-cleaning detergent used to cope with the salt spray has also been studied and results are attached. I hope you have enjoyed my study and explanation of the ocean."

What a farce! What a foolish explanation. Yet we have those people among us today who forget that the Bible exists only to bring us to the Lord Jesus Christ. He is the ocean beyond the window. The young man receiving the above letter might decide that seeing the ocean was not worth a trip to the Atlantic Coast. If it were only to study the window through which the ocean might be seen, surely he would be right. Is it not possible that many spend so much time on the Bible itself that they fail to look through the Bible to see the wonderful person of Jesus Christ, Savior and Redeemer of the world? The Bible leads to Him who is the way, truth, and life, and He leads those who find Him into the mainstream of life to bring meaning and dignity to it and the people who stand in need of that dignity before God and man.

There Is a Time
for Bible Reading

A chaplain on the battlefield came to a wounded man lying on the ground. "Would you like me to read you something from the Book—the Bible?" he asked the soldier. "I'm so thirsty," replied the man; "I would rather have a drink of water." Quickly as he could the chaplain brought the water. Then the soldier asked, "Could you put something under my head?" The chaplain took off his light outer coat, rolled it, and put it gently under the soldier's head for a pillow. "Now," said the soldier, "if I had something over me! I am very cold." There was only one thing the chaplain could do. He took off his other coat, and spread it over the soldier. The wounded man looked up into his face, and said gratefully, "Thank you." Then he added further, "If there is anything in that Book in your hand that makes a man do to another what you have done for me, please read it to me."

How quickly the chaplain had sized up the situation! What a terrible "let-down" would have taken place had he insisted on giving the wounded soldier the "Bread of Life" and the "warmth of the gospel" through the reading of the Scriptures. At that very moment the most important thing was to make the gospel of Jesus Christ come "alive" through the practical application of loving concern for the physical needs of the wounded soldier. What a golden opportunity for the chaplain to immediately become the "serving church" in the very real area of life. Also, what an opportunity to show love and the desire to serve the Lord and Savior. "Truly, I say to you, as you did it to one of the least of these my brethren, you did it to me" (Matt. 25:40). The motivation for the acts of kindness gave "life" to the words of Christ. Because of the chaplain's actions the wounded man desired to hear from the Book of Life.

We must ask ourselves the question, "Am I only "reading" the Bible or by knowledge gained from my reading can I apply God's Word to my daily life?" Standing on the threshold of the birthday of Jesus Christ the Savior of the world, are we filled with the compassion to needy man that gave Him impetus and direction to enter into this world scene? Do we have such insight into the problems of humanity, by the grace of God, that we can lay aside our "reading" and entertaining "activity"? Surely we find the meaning to divine-human relationships in the Bible; surely we learn of the joyful destiny found in Christianity in His Word. There is a time for reading, but there is also a time for action!

Christ, the Good Shepherd

How to Tell a Real Shepherd

An interesting story is told about a party of tourists traveling on the way to Palestine. The guide in charge of the tour was describing some of the quaint customs of the East. Among the unusual sights one might see in that land, the guide reminded them, was the manner by which a shepherd took care of his flock. "Now," he said, "you are accustomed to seeing the shepherd following his sheep through the English lanes and byways. In the East, however, things are different, for the shepherd always leads the way, going on before the flock. And the sheep follow him, for they know his voice."

The party reached Palestine, and, to the amusement of the tourists, almost the first sight to meet their eyes was that of a flock of sheep being driven along by a man. The guide was astonished and immediately made it his business to accost the shepherd. "How is it that you are driving these sheep?" he asked. "I have always been told that the Eastern shepherd leads his sheep." The man, driving the sheep, looked at him and answered, "You are quite right, sir. The shepherd does lead his sheep. But you see, I'm not the shepherd, I'm the butcher."

Scripture is filled with examples of the Savior being known as the great and loving Shepherd. His followers are naturally the sheep that are cared for by Him. One of the most well-known and well-loved bits of the Bible is the twenty-third psalm that begins, "The Lord is my Shepherd." In the Gospel of John we read these words of Jesus, "I am the good shepherd; I know my own and my own know me, as the Father knows me and I know the Father; and I lay down my life for the sheep" (10:14-15). This has always been a comfort and assurance for anyone who knows what it means to be able to trust fully and completely. There is no fear in the life of the "sheep" because he knows he will be led in paths that are for his good, both here in the present and hereafter in eternity.

One is to remember there is no such thing as being "driven" into the presence and love of Almighty God. But one is to constantly remember that, knowing the voice of One who calls, he can follow in safety and joy. Know the Shepherd and follow Him!

Christ, the Good Shepherd

Lost!

It was one of those dark winter nights. Freezing rain was turning to snow. The temperature was rapidly falling, and there was nothing more inviting than the warm glow of the fire before which two men were sitting. Suddenly there was a knock at the front door. The farmer went to answer it, as the rest of the household had gone to bed for the night. Returning to the other man, the farmer stated simply that someone had informed him that his sheep were missing from the field where they had been placed by him. He just had to go out into the bitter cold and find them. Preparing themselves, the two men took lanterns and went out into the darkness.

In one of the hedges of the field where the sheep had been left, the farmer discovered what he called "a bolting hole." A strong sheep had worked its way through at that point, and all the other sheep had followed. It was either in the third or fourth field that the two men came up with the straying animals. They found them scattered over the pasture. No two of them seemed to be together. Each had chosen its own course, regardless of the path another had taken. All were lost alike. Each had followed his own desires!

In the prophet Isaiah's book we read, "All we like sheep have gone astray; we have turned every one to his own way" (53:6a). It is very apparent that there are many people who use the "bolting hole" and wander from the safety and assurance of all that God would do for them. The natural pride of the individual encourages him to turn to his own way, his own feelings, his own ideas of what life is all about. Unfortunately, the individual becomes as the lost sheep of the story. He finds himself alone—lost; or he finds himself with others—also lost, having no hope for the future and no assurance that it is well with him.

The same Jesus Christ who has said, "I am the Way," also has called himself the "Good Shepherd." As one that is sincerely interested in us as precious, He wants to lead us in safe paths, keep watch over us, and have us feel the protection of His "field"—His own church. We are reminded again and again, especially during the season of Lent, just how much He does love us and to what extent He went that we might be His, now and forever. The cross is the symbol of that love. Without the Christ of the cross we are lost!

Christmas

Contemplating Christmas

It happened in a small church one Christmas Eve. After the carols had been sung, the meditation given by the pastor, and the Service of Candlelighting had been effectively presented in the darkened sanctuary, the pastor announced there would be a period of silent prayer—followed by the Christmas offering. Just before the offering plates were passed among the congregation, one serious and somewhat sad looking woman turned to her husband and whispered, "Dad, I know our son John was killed in service just last week, but let us give to the Lord a goodly portion of our income in thanksgiving that He, by His birth and life and death, made our son His child eternally. Let's show our thanks for the faith John had in his Savior." Behind this couple another man and woman overheard the whispered conversation. "Bill," said the woman behind the couple, "let us also give a sizeable gift to the Lord in behalf of our son, Bill, Jr." "Why?" said Bill, "nothing has happened to him, he hasn't even been wounded in service." "That's just it," replied the thankful mother, "just think how much we can rejoice and be happy. Can we do less?"

There are many in our community today busily engaged in Christmas activity and preparation. Stores will be crowded by last-minute shoppers. Goodies will have been carefully made or purchased at specialty shops. Living in and surrounded by abundance, many will be totally unaware of their blessings. But there are those who know the heaviness of heart that comes with misfortune and tragedy. Years ago an article appeared in the *New York Herald Tribune* that was clipped out by Alexander Woollcott

15

and became one of his favorite pieces of simple poetry. Written by an unknown author, it said:

> Christmas is a bitter day
> For mothers who are poor,
> The wistful eyes of children
> Are daggers to endure.
>
> Though shops are crammed with playthings
> Enough for everyone,
> If a mother's purse is empty
> There might as well be none.
>
> My purse is full of money
> But I cannot buy a toy;
> Only a wreath of holly
> For the grave of my little boy.

But there is more to Christmas! Read the story of hope—Luke 2:8-14.

Christmas

That's What I Want for Christmas

Alan Hynd, writing in the magazine *Coronet* several years ago, asked for the following gift: "Be sure, Saint Nicholas, to leave the Star of Bethlehem for the Peacemakers, so that its light, out of the East, will make them wise men, and compassionate and humble. Leave them, too, the gift of the spirit of brotherhood, so that they will know that we are all the children of God, whether bronze or white, yellow or brown.

"Leave tolerance for those who dwell in the halls of persecution. Shower upon the fighting men the gift of eternal gratitude. To all cynics leave the road to yesterday when, like Little Boy Blue, they dreamed of gingerbread castles and rock candy mountains.

"In the dark valleys of doubt, from the Levant to the China Sea, leave trust, all wrapped in bright cellophane. And in the ghettos of the earth leave that most precious of all gifts—hope. Leave unselfishness for Capital, and leave the just rewards of ambition for Saturday's Children—the children of Labor."

The same desire is certainly appropriate for today's world. If only the Prince of Peace could find a welcome in the hearts and lives of those who are engaged in an endless struggle brought about by greed and assumed unfairness. If only that One who is called "The Light of the World" could shine into the dark recesses of sin, arrogance, pride, and selfishness. If only Emmanuel (God with us) would be allowed to dwell with us, what a glorious season this could be and remain. However, John wrote, at the very beginning of his Gospel, "The true light that enlightens every man was coming into the world. He was in the world, and the world was made through him, yet the world knew him not" (John 1:9-10). What a terrible indictment—"The world knew him not!" But the marvel of divine love is shown through the fact that God has not turned His back upon man. This season is the reminder to each and every one that "God so loved the world that He gave His only Son. . . ." He gave to us, and for us, His most cherished possession—Himself!

Even as it has been hoped that the Star of Bethlehem would lead men to the manger of the Babe and thereby reveal wisdom, so also we hope that man might truly become wise in God's sight. If the Christchild is seen with the eyes of the heart and kept there, that is all I want for Christmas!

Courage

It Takes Courage to Suffer

He was only a little tyke who came walking up the aisle of the gathered assembly. He had little fat, brown legs, and there was serious determination in his eyes. The speaker stopped and looked at him. The people who had gathered together were quiet as death. "You asked what I would have done if I had been in the crowd when Jesus fell under the weight of His cross." He looked up earnestly at the preacher. "Please, sir, I would have helped carry it." He was a Mexican lad eight years of age. His father was a miner and his mother was an outcast from decent society. The story of Simon of Cyrene had been presented, and when the speaker had asked the audience to determine in their own hearts their reaction to that scene, little Pedro had moved to the front of the building. The speaker lifted his arm and cried somewhat threateningly: "Yes, and if you had helped Him to carry His cross, the cruel Roman soldiers would have beaten down across your back with their whips until the blood ran down to your heels!" The boy never flinched. Meeting the speaker's look with one of cool courage, he gritted through clenched teeth: "I don't care. I would have helped Him carry it just the same." An admirable statement of heroism, but one that had not too much meaning. After all, anyone could say that in the safety of twenty centuries removed from the event.

Two weeks later, at the close of another worship service, held in the same building, the same preacher stood at the door, greeting people as they left. When Pedro, the small boy with the big testimony, came by, he was affectionately patted on the back. He shrank from the preacher with a little crying sob. "Don't do that. My back is sore." The preacher stood in astonishment. He had barely touched the boy's shoulders. Taken into the cloak room and having his shirt removed from his body, the boy showed ugly, bloody welts criss-crossed from neck to waist. "Who did that?" the preacher cried in anger and shock. "Mother did it. She whipped me because I came to church," the boy answered. His bravery and willingness to "carry the cross" were not idle boastings.

Our Lord said at one time, "Blessed are you when men revile you and persecute you and utter all kinds of evil against you falsely on my account. Rejoice and be glad, for your reward is great in heaven, for so men persecuted the prophets who were before you" (Matt. 5:11-12). Should we not take Him at His word and be courageous enough to stand up for Him?

Dependence on God

Is It the Right Stone?

Some years ago there came to Los Angeles, the great metropolis of Southern California, a so-called human fly. It was announced that on a certain day he would climb up the face of one of the large department store buildings, and long before the appointed time thousands of eager spectators were gathered to see him perform the seemingly impossible feat.

Slowly and carefully he mounted aloft, now clinging to a window ledge, now to a jutting brick, again to a cornice. Up and up he went, against apparently insurmountable difficulties. At last he was nearing the top. He was seen to feel to right and left and above his head for something firm enough to support his weight, to carry him further. And soon he seemed to spy what looked like a grey bit of stone or discolored brick protruding from the smooth wall. He reached for it, but it was just beyond him. He ventured all on a spring-like movemeni, grasped the protuberance and before the horrified eyes of the spectators, fell to the ground and was broken to pieces. In his dead hand was found a spider's web! What he evidently mistook for solid stone or brick turned out to be nothing but dried froth!

What a lesson for those who will only stop and think. Climbing higher and higher in the world of man there are those who seem to carefully pick their way and who are making strides to the pinnacle of success. The "window ledges" of human knowledge and skill; the "jutting bricks" of influential friends and inside information; the "cornices" of conniving and domineering—these seem to carry a man to within reach of his goal. As he carefully makes his way there seems to be but one more stone to grasp. With defiant desperation he makes his move! That which seemed to be a strong, sizeable rock turns out to be "dried froth"! But then it is too late.

While human efforts are to be used and opportunities accepted and challenges met, it is equally true that no one knows, understands, or has meaning to his life if he ignores the only solid "rock" that one can find—the God-man, Jesus Christ. Ignoring the plain and lasting "Rock" man fails miserably. Luke's Gospel reminds us that "the very stone which the builders rejected has become the head of the corner" (Luke 20:17). There can be no life, no living, no goal met, that will continue to all eternity if the Rock of Ages is not seen as that upon which man can only find assurance of success. As we make our way in life carefully and cautiously, let us always reach for the right "Stone."

Dependence on God

There Was No Connection!

Several years ago a United Press report from San Antonio, Texas, stated that a hospital over thirty-five years old had an expensive firefighting system on all floors. This system, one of the best of its time, was installed for the safety of the patients in the hospital. However, an investigation and assessment of the value of the system took place and it was discovered that it had never been connected with the city's water main. The pipe that led from the firefighting system extended four feet underground—and there it stopped! An appropriation was immediately made, of course, to hook the hospital's system to the city water pipes. A tragedy had been averted.

In just such a way there are those living in the world today who are relying upon personal character, formal church membership, and/or benevolent contributions to make themselves feel worthy in the sight of a sinless God. Yet the Lord Himself has said, "I am the vine, you are the branches. He who abides in me, and I in him, he it is that bears much fruit, for apart from me you can do nothing" (John 15:5). If there is no connection with the divine power and force found in Jesus Christ, any attempt to "do good" amounts to nothing more than a humanism that loses its effectiveness.

The reason there is so much fear and uncertainty, in efforts that rely solely on human activity, is that there is both a conscious and unconscious realization that the efforts of men are doomed to failure because of basic selfishness and self-centeredness. No one, with the spirit of Christ absent, can maintain a full and free concern for relationships that will be in harmony with the divine will of God. Placing the pipe into the ground without any connection to the source of power is not enough. To be used effectively, energy must flow through the "system." There is a constant challenge issued by the Lord to examine and reexamine the activities of each person's life. Is there just the outward motion that make things "look good" without any tie-in to the power and strength of the Lord, or is there really and honestly a connection that makes activity glorify the one and only living God?

Discontent

Sometime ago there appeared in a newspaper a cartoon showing two fields divided by a fence. Both fields were about the same size, and each had plenty of the same kind of grass, green and lush. In each field there was a mule, and each mule had his head through the fence eating grass from the other mule's pasture. All around each mule in his own field was plenty of grass, yet the grass in the other field seemed greener or fresher, although it was harder to get. And in the process the mules were caught in the wires and were unable to extricate themselves. The cartoonist put just one word at the bottom of the picture—"DISCONTENT!"

There are a great number of people who are like those mules. Discontented with their lot in life, although having sufficient "things" in this life, these same people are dissatisfied and unappreciative of what is theirs. Humanity, generally, thinks it would be much happier if it could have what is in the other's "field." At the same time there is an ignoring, or an unmindfulness, of what is at hand for one's own benefit. A little verse helps us to see the foolishness and sinfulness of discontent:

> As a rule a man's a fool;
> When it's hot, he wants it cool;
> When it's cool, he wants it hot;
> Always wanting what is not.

Perhaps it wouldn't be so bad if discontent remained just that —discontent, but there are several other sins that develop from it. One sees another who has more and is seemingly living a comfortable and luxurious life. Others apparently are "getting ahead" and seem to be more popular. Bigger houses to live in, newer and more expensive cars, custom-made and original clothes, better positions—all these things fall into the hands of those who have no more right to them than the discontented one. Theft, meanness, selfishness, impatience, and broken homes result from one's discontent. The joy of living is lost and tempers flare up. God's Word says, "Be content with such things as you have" (Heb. 13:5 KJV). There is no need to be resigned. There is nothing that says we cannot continue to make an effort, proper and lawful, to rise to higher positions. But in the meantime we are to be conscious of that which we already have through the love of God. Unhappiness and violence are the results of ungodly and bitter discontent.

Eternal Destiny

Well Done—Enter

"His master said to him, 'Well done, good and faithful servant; you have been faithful over a little, I will set you over much; enter into the joy of your master' " (Matt. 25:23). It seems there was a lowly workman who helped in the building of the great Cathedral of

Cologne. When the massive structure was being dedicated, he among the huge crowd was so very proud. Someone asked him why he was feeling so important and he told this person that he was responsible for the painting found on the walls and ceiling. "How can this be?" he was asked. "Who are you?" "Only a hod carrier," he replied, "but it was the brick and stone that I carried that was used as a foundation that made all the rest possible." "Only a hod carrier." How often we deprecate the position we hold in life. We look about and see others in positions of greater responsibility, greater glamor, greater prominence, and immediately we feel useless. Perhaps we even resent the fact that we have not attained a position of higher authority that demands respect from our fellowman.

Instead of constantly grumbling about the "tools" God has given us, why should we not determine that we will use what we have to the fullest and best of our talent? Why should we not trust in the wisdom of the Lord and say with the poet,

> While some with talents five begun,
> He started out with only one.
> "With this," he said, "I'll do my best
> And trust the Lord to do the rest."

There are so many "small" but important jobs for each of us. A friendly smile or a word of encouragement to one "down in the dumps"; engaging in the exciting game of "fair play" among the nations and races of our world; speaking out against the widespread immorality now enveloping our country. Sincerity is the only talent needed—sincerity and a willingness to be guided by Him "from whom all blessings flow." If we show ourselves trustworthy over the little things of life we will hear the Lord's benediction: "Well done . . . enter."

Faith

Playing for Peanuts

A woman visiting the Philadelphia Zoo one day noticed that someone had slipped a pair of dice into the monkey cage. She complained to the zoo keeper that the monkeys had the dice and were gambling. At first the man ignored the woman, but when she became quite insistent, he replied, "Lady, those monkeys are not gambling, they are playing for peanuts."

How often must the Christian be accused of "playing for peanuts" while there are worlds to be won and when there are future generations at stake. Mankind cries out for relief and redemption. Nations are anxious and concerned about survival. Individuals seek answers to basic questions of life. And while these terrifying things are causing men and women to cringe and plead for help, the Christian, preoccupied with the trivia of life, "fiddles while Rome burns," and "plays for peanuts." If the church is failing, if the message of reconciliation is ineffective, and if the word of the Lord is not being heard, is it because of stubborn unbelief and the unwillingness of the follower of the Lord to accept the direction God would give in Jesus Christ?

We read in Matthew 13:58, "And he did not do many mighty works there, because of their unbelief." If the Lord is Lord and if He is "the way, the truth, and the life," then let us stand before the world as a living testimony of what the new life is and what it can do—bring peace, love, understanding, and compassion.

Faith in Christ is a venture—a grand and glorious adventure. There are risks involved in expressing that faith by more than mere words. Faith is action. Faith is interest and concern for all mankind. Faith is siding with justice and speaking out against the persecution of minorities and the withholding of rights that belong to all people regardless of race, color, or creed. Faith is reflecting Christ and His eternal promises. There is no time to "play for peanuts." Let us give Jesus the chance to do "mighty works" through and in us. Act as a "little Christ" by word and deed. Proclaim His wonderful gift of grace—salvation full and free in the God that became man that man might come to God fully pardoned and saved.

Faith

Stop Struggling!

One day a small boy had ventured too far out into the lake where he had been wading. Over his head in the water, he began to struggle but was unable to reach safe ground. On the shore, his mother, in an agony of fright and grief, called out for someone to save her drowning son. At her side stood a strong man, seemingly indifferent to the boy's fate. Again and again the mother appealed to him to help save the young lad. But he made no move. By and by the desperate struggles of the boy began to lessen. He was losing strength. Presently he rose to the surface, weak and helpless. At that moment the strong man leaped into the stream and brought the boy in safety to the shore. "Why didn't you save my boy sooner?" cried the now grateful mother. "Madam, I could not save your boy as long as he struggled. He would have dragged us both to certain death. But when he grew weak and ceased to struggle, then it was easy to save him."

How like the drowning boy are those dissatisfied and guilt-stricken people of this earth. Struggling to find relief of conscience, attacking the problems of this life with insufficient spiritual ability, flailing aimlessly in the "waters" of trouble, failures, and sin, the man and woman of today, as in days past, fear for their soul life. Knowing God is righteous and holy, natural man finds he is incapable of meeting the just demands of God. Man forgets that to be justified, to be considered "right" in God's sight, he must accept the gift of God. We read, "By grace are ye saved, through faith; and that not of yourself; it is the gift of God" (Eph. 2:8 KJV). No amount of personal "struggle" can bring assurance of rightness with God. No sincere effort, no matter how diligently performed, can solve man's basic problem—separation from God because of sin. Only the admission of imperfection on man's part, and his total reliance on divine love, found in Jesus Christ alone, can bring about restoration. When one no longer "struggles" on his own to save himself the Son of God is able to accomplish His saving purpose.

Many a person, sincerely concerned about his spiritual welfare, has attempted to live the perfect life. Many a person has dedicated himself to "doing good" and "following the Moral Code." Many a person has found himself on the brink of futility and failure. But many a man, in just such a position, has found peace and assurance for this life and the life to come by relying on the gift of God—Jesus Christ. Why not stop struggling with self-righteousness?

Faithfulness

"We Died Here Fighting"

In the pass of Thermopylae, in the country of Greece, there stands a monument, world renowned, erected to Leonidas and his valiant three hundred. It bears the inscription: "Go, stranger, and tell at Sparta that we died here fighting to the last in obedience to our laws," and it commemorates that thrilling event when Leonidas with his three hundred successfully held the pass of Thermopylae against tremendous odds until betrayed into the hands of the enemy. Thus this monument bears magnificent witness to the quality of loyalty or steadfastness. Even so God demands of His people faithfulness unto death. In Revelation 2:10 we read: "Be thou faithful unto death, and I will give thee a crown of life" (KJV).

In this day and age the Christian is challenged every bit as much as in the past to bear a loyal witness to the principles of Jesus Christ. Obedience to the laws of both God and man are being violated. Gross immorality is almost an accepted pattern of life and, tragically, is not recognized. Stealing property is still punished—sometimes—but stealing the dignity and worthwhileness of the individual goes unnoticed and unpunished. Blasphemy causes the "better" educated and socially oriented community to shudder, but "Nigger," "Kike," "Hunky," are terms that can be used to define the "upstarts" and "troublemakers."

Will it become necessary for the Christian to endure the persecution of the "Establishment" because of ideals and steadfastness and loyalty to Christ's understanding of the worth of man in any economic or social strata? Are we in danger of another Thermopylae? If so, who is liable to betray us?

The Christian banner is emblazoned with the words "Justice," "Peace," "Righteousness," "Reconciliation," "Redemption," and "Brotherhood." It is to be carried into the world with bravery and courage. The Law of God and the law of man desire all men, everywhere, to "fight the good fight of faith." Can equality and love prevail? Let us see in the life of Christ that example that can lead to honest tranquility and lasting peace between peoples of all nations and races. Let us pray that it will not be necessary to die "fighting to the last," but let us also pray we may see the right and pursue it even if "we died here fighting."

False Guidance

Don't Be Misdirected!

The famous Billy Sunday once told this story. There was a terrible blizzard raging over the eastern part of the States, making more and more difficult the progress of a train that was slowly forcing its way along. Among the passengers was a woman with a child. She was much concerned lest she should not get off at the right station. A gentleman, seeing her anxiety, said: "Do not worry, I know the road well, and I will tell you when you come to your station."

In due course, the train stopped at the station before the one at which the woman wanted to get off. "The next station will be yours, ma'am," said the gentleman. Then they went on, and in a few minutes the train stopped again. "Now is your time, ma'am; get out quickly," he said. The woman took up her child and, thanking the man, left the train. At the next stop, the brakeman called out the name of the station where the woman had wished to get off.

"You have already stopped at this station," called the man to the brakeman. "No sir," he replied, "something was wrong with the engine and we stopped for a few minutes to repair it." "O my God!" cried the passenger, "I put that woman off in the storm when the train stopped between stations!" Afterwards, they found her with her child in her arms. Both were frozen to death! It was the terrible and tragic consequence of wrong direction being given!

How many times have we been given the wrong direction, information, or assurance. Following advice given, we have discovered we were traveling in the wrong direction, or that a detour had been set up that caused us to retrace our steps. Looking at ourselves, must we not admit there have been times when we told someone, with a most positive manner, our thinking, only to find out later that it was wrong! Some of these errors can be corrected without too much danger and with a minimum amount of inconvenience. Some little time was lost and that was all.

Think of the everlasting damage that is done to the person who is told there are other ways to save his soul and give meaning to life. Jesus Christ was very explicit when He said to doubting Thomas, "I am the way, and the truth, and the life; no one comes to the Father, but by me" (John 14:6). Dare we take chances on our eternal destiny? Dare we believe that man has improved on God's way? Do we want to risk our souls on foolish, human invention? Life, now and forever, is too precious. Don't be misdirected!

"Where's the Water?"

A man by the name of Sir Samuel Baker relates the following incident: "Many years ago, when the Egyptian troops first conquered Nubia, a regiment was destroyed by thirst in crossing the Nubian desert. The men, being upon a limited allowance of water, suffered from extreme thirst; and, deceived by the appearance of a mirage that exactly resembled a beautiful lake, they insisted on being taken to its banks by the Arab guide. It was in vain that the guide assured them that the lake was unreal, and he refused to lose the precious time by wandering from his course. Words led to blows, and he was killed by the soldiers, whose lives depended upon his guidance. The whole regiment turned from the track and rushed toward the welcome waters. Thirsty and faint, over the burning sands they hurried; heavier and heavier their footsteps became, hotter and hotter their breath as deeper they pushed into the desert, farther and farther from the lost track, where the pilot lay in his blood; and still the mocking spirits of the desert, the fantasies of the mirage, led them on, and the lake glistening in the sunshine, tempted them to bathe in the cool waters, close to their eyes, but never at their lips. At length the delusion vanished—the fatal lake had turned to burning sand! Raging thirst and horrible despair! The pathless desert and the murdered guide! Lost! Lost! All lost! Not a man ever left the desert, but they were subsequently discovered, parched and withered corpses, by the Arabs sent out upon the search."

What a tragic story of desire overcoming discretion, of self-will rather than a secure way! Failing to follow one who knew the correct path to safety and security, the soldiers of the party chose to dash after that which was only a mirage. What a loss of manpower! What an unhappy and tortuous end for each one concerned! And even more so in the battle of life and the seeking of a meaningful goal, is the eternal tragedy of those who refuse to listen to the word of the Son of God, who, becoming the Son of man, would lead to "fountains of living water." In the great revelation picture, the angel gives assurance to those who seek the same "living water." He says, speaking for the Savior-King, "To the thirsty I will give water without price from the fountain of the water of life" (Rev. 21:6). There is a thirst for life's meaning. There is opportunity to slake one's thirst. But it does not come from the mirages of human thought and drive. It comes only from the Lord. He is the water of life. That's where the water is!

ㄹㄴ Nω δ]

Father's Day

In the *Diary of Brooks Adams* is a note about a special day when he was eight years old. He wrote, "Went fishing with my father; the most glorious day of my life," and through the next forty years there were constant references to that day and the influence it had on his life.

Brooks's father was Charles Francis Adams, Abraham Lincoln's ambassador to Great Britain. He also had a note in his diary about the same day. It simply said, "Went fishing with my son: a day wasted."

As we look forward to celebrating the day that honors fathers, we cannot overlook the fact that the "head of the house" still exerts great influence on his children. Unknown to him, those that are in the household are greatly affected by his words, his actions, and his deeds.

Since its first publication many years ago, over thirty million copies of Charles M. Sheldon's book *In His Steps* have been sold. In his famous book Sheldon gives this testimony: "In a log house on the prairie my father taught me to love the Bible. After breakfast every day the family moved over into the end of the room we called the parlor and had family worship. Each of us had a Bible of his own. Father would read two verses out loud from the chapter of the day, then Mother would read two verses, and each one of us two verses. Before five years were over we read the whole Bible five times. I think I am the only man living who has heard the whole Bible read aloud five times. We never skipped, not even those long lists of worthies who begat one another. The minute we finished Revelation, father calmly turned back to Genesis and we went at it again. I want to repeat that my father taught me to love the Bible as the greatest book in the world.

"At the family worship after the Bible reading we would sing a hymn and then all kneel down while father offered the morning prayer. We are Scotch-Irish, and naturally father prayed as long as he liked. And he would often pray for us by name.

"When I finally left home to go down East to college, I would often be tempted to do what some of the college boys did—swear, play cards for money, and go downtown at night where I ought not to go. Then just as I was about to give way to my desires, I would hear my father's morning prayer in the log house."

Sounds rather naive, doesn't it! But how much more respect for person and property we would have if more fathers would use their Christian influence.

Forgiveness

Are You Able to Actually Forgive?

Of all English kings, Richard seems to have been the bravest. History tells us that he was a great warrior, and because of his daring and prowess upon the battlefield he was surnamed Coeur-de-Lion, or the Lion-hearted. Like many another brave man, he was also very generous, and able to forgive wrongs. It is recorded that, when his treacherous brother John, who had tried to rob him of his crown, pleaded for mercy, he said, "I forgive him, and I hope to forget his injuries as easily as he will forget my pardon." After he had reigned about ten years, one of his French vassals, Vidomar, Viscount of Limoges, rebelled against him. Richard at once marched his army against him, and beseiged him in his castle of Chaluz.

During the siege, with his usual disregard of danger, Richard approached very near the castle walls, almost wholly unattended. Seeing this, a young man, named Bertrand de Gurdun, fitted an arrow to his bow and took aim at the king. The arrow pierced Richard's left shoulder and proved to be a fatal wound. While the king lay in his tent, the castle was taken and Bertrand made captive; heavily ironed, he was led to the bedside of the suffering and dying monarch. Richard looked calmly into his face and said, "Youth, I forgive you my death." Then turning to his soldiers standing by he said, "Let him go free, and give him a hundred shillings." Although having dealt the death blow to King Richard, the young soldier, because of the forgiveness granted by his victim, was allowed to continue life in freedom.

It is the mark of a truly great man to forgive totally! Rather than retribution and vengeance, if the spirit of forgiveness were in evidence certainly there would be more love. For those who believe in God's love, as shown in Jesus Christ, the words of the Savior become a guide and directive in life, for He has said, "For if you forgive men their trespasses, your heavenly Father also will forgive you; but if you do not forgive men their trespasses, neither will your Father forgive your trespasses" (Matt. 6:14-15). When one compares himself to the perfectness of God and realizes his own personal need for forgiving understanding, he will be more quickly desirous of forgiving those whom he feels have wronged him. Are you able to do so? Only one strengthened by divine forgiveness can. Have you sought it in order to be able to do it?

Forgiveness

God Can't Always Forgive!

A man named Samuel Holmes, who was in the Frankfort, Kentucky, jail undergoing punishment for murder, received a visit from an old schoolfellow of his, Lucien Young. The Kentucky legislature, having recorded some years previously its appreciation of Young's condition, made an appeal to Governor Blackburn for Holmes's pardon. The governor, remembering his brave action, relented and signed the pardon for Young's sake.

With the document in his pocket, Young hastened back to the prison to tell the good news to his friend. Before intimating, however, that he had power to make him a free man, Young commenced a conversation. After talking awhile upon other subjects, he finally said: "Sam, if you were turned loose and fully pardoned, what would be the first thing you would do?" The convict quickly responded. "I would go to Lancaster, and kill Judge Owsley and a man who was a witness against me."

Young did not utter a word, but turned mournfully away, went outside the prison wall, and taking the pardon from his pocket, he tore it into fragments. This is the story as it was told in the *Richmond Register*. Holmes lost his pardon simply because he would not forgive. He had no penitence with which to meet pardon and godly sorrow with which to respond to the offer of undeserved mercy.

In the Gospel of Matthew, Jesus makes a statement, after teaching His disciples the Lord's Prayer. He says: "For if you forgive men their trespasses, your heavenly Father also will forgive you; but if you do not forgive men their trespasses, neither will your

Father forgive your trespasses" (6:14-15). Meaningful and effective forgiveness depends on the individual. God cannot, God will not forgive any who refuse to show mercy and forgiveness to others. It is dangerous to pray, "Forgive us our trespasses *as we forgive those who trespass against us"!*

If man would only realize what he is doing when bitterness, rancor, and hatred remain in his heart! If the individual person could only understand that the lack of charity and love keeps him at a distance from God! There may be lurking in the hearts of us deep and forboding thoughts about real or imagined acts against us by others. Do we harbor the notion of revenge, or are we honestly willing to forgive and seek complete forgiveness from God in Jesus Christ? Just remember, God can't always forgive! He expects man to reflect His willingness to reconcile.

Forgiveness

I Hurt

An anxious, worried father sat at the bedside of his six-year-old son who had just undergone emergency surgery. Concerned as only a father can be over a loved one, he had terrible thoughts creep into his mind. Why had not the doctor been called sooner? Why hadn't he suspected his son's trouble and not diagnosed it as a mere stomach ache? Why hadn't he taken his son to a medical authority who could have solved the problem? For over an hour these guilt feelings repeated themselves.

Soon after, a slight stirring of the boy in the bed brought the father closer. Seeing the boy's eyes slowly open, he bent over the child and heard him falteringly whisper, "Hold my hand, daddy, I hurt so bad." Reaching down he took the hand of the little fellow who smiled wanly and then went back to sleep. The father taking his cue from his son, closed his eyes and said quietly to our heavenly Father, "Hold my hand, Father, I hurt."

The psalmist cried out, "My eyes are toward thee, O Lord God; in thee I seek refuge; leave me not defenseless" (Ps. 141:8). It is with the same childlike confidence of the little boy in the hospital bed that the Christian knows he can ask to have his hand taken into the hand of God and thus be reassured that he is not alone, forsaken, or forgotten by God.

We "hurt" from the trials, troubles, and tears of this world. Racked by the "fever" of a guilty conscience, the spiritual pain sometimes seems more than we can bear. It is then the cry comes from our hearts, "Father, take my hand, I hurt." The most wonderful thing occurs. No temporary sedation is offered. The lasting comfort of His presence in Christ is ours. Sin, transgression of divine Law, brings grievous hurt. Sin, causing separation from heavenly love, causes anxiety and fear. Sin, opening the door to frustration, failure, and fears, brings despair. Sin hurts deep within the heart and soul. Coming to God, in Jesus' name, we need only confess our sins, seek forgiveness, and, believing, receive the loving hand of the Father. After He takes our hand we can assuredly say, "Thank you, my Father, I no longer hurt."

Fourth of July

What Do You Believe?

Several years ago, a student from the University of Wisconsin appeared on the steps of the state capitol reading the Declaration of Independence and asking passers-by to sign the document. But most of them refused. It was not long until the police appeared on the scene, for someone had phoned them that there was a Communist on the Capitol steps that should be taken into custody.

It seems the young student was seeking to bring to the attention of the general public something of the predicament of our nation today where the erosion of the foundations of our government are taking place at an alarming rate. There is such apathy and indifference toward the ideals that have made and preserved us as a nation that they are no longer even recognized by John Q. Public. And anyone who is interested in proclaiming them or propagating them is apt to be labeled a reactionary of some color or creed.

Many years ago, a great leader, of an equally great nation, spoke a farewell address to those he had loved and served. His earthly end was near at hand, and he used the occasion to point out some of the besetting sins of the nation and to challenge the citizenry to a renewed commitment to God so they might enter into the great inheritance that God had willed for them. The man was Joshua; the nation, Israel, of Old Testament times. What was said in part was this, ". . . fear the Lord, and serve him in sincerity and in faithfulness. . . . And if you be unwilling to serve the Lord, choose this day whom you will serve . . . but as for me and my house, we will serve the Lord" (Josh. 24:14-15).

We again are about to celebrate the Fourth of July, the anniversary of the independence of the nation we love. As loyal citizens we are asked to not only recall the blessings of "freedom, under God," but also to dedicate ourselves to a continuation of those principles we hold dear in our hearts. Even as in the days of Joshua of old, today there is need for voices to proclaim the fact that democracy, in all its real meaning, can only be had if individuals are willing to place the Lord in His rightful place. To serve the nation properly and usefully one must first dedicate himself to the God of peace.

The manifesto of the dignity of the individual originates within the mind of God. This great land of ours, to remain great, cannot blindly ignore Him and serve the gods of selfish ambitions. Each person must be granted the privileges that God Himself dictated. America, choose this day whom you shall serve!

Freedom in Christ

Released and Free!

Years ago the king of Abyssinia took a man by the name of Campbell, prisoner. He was a citizen of Great Britain. He was carried to the fortress of Magdala, and in the height of the mountains put in a dungeon. No cause was assigned for his confinement. After six months Great Britain found it out. They demanded an immediate release for their citizen. King Theodore refused to release him.

Within ten days, ten thousand soldiers were on shipboard, sailing down the coast. They disembarked and marched seven hundred miles under the blasting rays of a hot sun up the mountains to the dungeon where their subject was held prisoner. They gave battle, tore the gates down, and soon reached the prisoner, lifted him out and placed him on their shoulders and carried him all the way down the mountains and placed him on one of the big ocean vessels which sped him safely home. Ten thousand soldiers were employed in the release of one man. It took several months to release and return the prisoner. It cost the English government twenty-five million dollars to release that man! The entire government was interested and ready to help him. Through the combined efforts of the soldiers the man was released and freed.

The Christian belongs to a much better Kingdom where there is concern for the total being. Becoming a child of God means that no power can keep the individual in chains. Satan with all his hellish hordes cannot contain the real life of that one who has placed his trust in the only begotten of the Father from all eternity. Paul, speaking to the Galatians, says that ". . . when the time had fully come, God sent forth his Son, born of woman, born under the law, to redeem those who were under the law, so that we might receive adoption as sons" (4:4-5). This means all the power and might of heaven is directed against the evil forces in the world that would make man captive and separate him from the eternal love of God. Just as in some measure a real concerned government will protect its citizenry, in a full and divine measure, God goes "all out" to rescue the fallen and the captive. The Lord can, will, and does more for His own than any earthly power can do for any of its subjects.

Paul continues in the same letter to the Galatians by saying, "So through God you are no longer a slave but a son, and if a son then an heir" (4:7). What greater assurance is there for anyone? Sin has bound me, but by the grace of God, and the activity of His Son, I can say, "I am released and free!

Generosity

Stretch It a Little

It happened at the turn of the century when blacksmiths' shops were common and patronized by those who owned horses and depended upon the artistry of the smithy to repair worn tools. One spring morning the head of the house invited his small son to go with him to Old Man Trussel's shop to pick up a rake and hoe that had been fixed. Entering the shop, the father and son saw them standing in the corner, fixed like new. Father handed over a silver dollar for the repair work, but the blacksmith refused to take it. "No," he said, "there's no charge for that little job." The man insisted that he take pay, still extending to him the dollar. The young boy, watching the transaction, was very impressed with both action and word. Later in life he commented, "If I live a thousand years, I'll never forget that humble yet great man's reply to my father. He said to my dad, 'Ed, can't you let a man do something now and then—just to stretch his soul?' "

One of the tragedies of modern living is that so few people are inclined to "stretch their souls." Everything done seems to have price tags labeled on the efforts. Charity and the desire to aid just for the sake of helping one's fellowman has gone down the drain in a materialistic age. Yet Scripture tells us "it is more blessed to give than to receive."

What the down-to-earth blacksmith said (". . . let a man do something now and then—just to stretch his soul") is the plea of today's concerned person who begs for greater "involvement" on the part of the members of society. We know that Jesus Christ of Nazareth, was called "The Man for Others." His entire earthly life was given over to "stretching his soul." Whenever the opportunity presented itself, the Lord was aiding the less fortunate, the disturbed, the disappointed, and the hopeless. Today, in spite of many programs to establish security for all men, there are those who live in areas of helplessness and hopelessness. In this area of life we can enter. Figuratively, we can repair "the hoes and the rakes" of disillusionment and defeat. The reward for a spiritual and special concern is the knowledge that we have some small part in attempting to advance the dignity of all people, both for time and eternity. This should be the joyful burden of a Christian's life. Payment for every action on our part makes life a small business transaction that leads ultimately to bankruptcy of life. Isn't it worth the effort to be about doing something for the sake of someone else and then refuse payment? Try following the example of the dignified blacksmith who found satisfaction in "stretching his soul."

God's Care

He Was There

In the pioneer days of our country, there was a boy whose home was situated in the backwoods. A school had been opened some miles away from where the boy lived. Part of the way to the school led through a dense forest. The boy's father was a strong, brave backwoodsman. He wanted his son to grow up to be strong and brave. So he told his son that he would have to go to school alone!

When the boy walked through the dark forest, he always expected to meet a bear or some wild Indians.

With the passing of the days and weeks, his fear subsided. Then, one day, late in the afternoon, he saw a great bear standing right in the pathway! The bear growled and glowered at the boy. The boy stood motionless, filled with fear. Even if he had run, it would have done no good, for the bear would have outrun him. As he stood there, a shot rang out. The bear fell dead. Then from the bushes, the father emerged. "It's all right, son. I've been with you all the time. Every morning I have followed you to school, and every afternoon I have been in the shadows watching you. I kept myself hidden from you because I wanted you to learn to be brave!"

There are times in every person's life when danger stares him in the face. Sometimes it is not danger of a physical nature but, rather, danger far more serious, with eternal consequences. The greatest danger anyone meets is that of being tempted to stray from all that is morally good and God-pleasing. Although His presence is unseen, nevertheless, the Lord God has assured that one who places his trust in Him, "Fear not; for I am with thee" (Gen. 26:24 KJV). This knowledge of God's unseen presence gives those who trust in Him courage, confidence, and comfort. Someone penned these words:

> God is before me, He will be my Guide,
> God is behind me, no ill can betide,
> God is beside me, to comfort and cheer,
> God is around me, so why should I fear?

Much danger is found in the world in which we live. With life so uncertain, with violence everywhere, with life offered at, and on, the altar of lust for power and prestige, certainly one needs the assurance that he is not "going it alone." Trust, believe, and know that He is there (meaning, wherever you may be).

God's Care

Never Really Alone

There was once a small family of three: father, mother, and a sweet little daughter, age three. The family was closely knit, and although there was not a great deal of material wealth, they experienced that oneness that comes from love, kindness, and consideration. It was a home that knew what God-love and God-living was all about. Sudden sorrow struck the home when the beautiful young wife was killed in an automobile accident. It appeared that all the light had gone out for the father and husband. The night after the funeral the man was putting his little daughter to bed, and with awkward fingers was buttoning her sleeping garment when the lights went out all over the house. He suspected that a fuse had blown out in the basement, and said to the child, "Papa will be right back; you lie still and wait here." But she, frightened at the thought of being left alone, pleaded that he take her with him, so he picked her up in his arms and groped through the darkened hallway and down the stairs. The child snuggled in his arms for a while in silence; but as they entered the basement she tightened her arms about his neck, and said, "It's awfully dark; but I'm not afraid, because my papa is here!" He buried his face in the baby's hair and wept, as he said, "Yes, dear, it is dark indeed; but I also am not afraid because *our* Father is here!"

Sometimes we live through dark days and nights. We are so taken up with personal problems and worries we forget the assurance given to us by the living God who says, "Fear not, for I have redeemed you; I have called you by name, you are mine. When you pass through the waters I will be with you; and through the rivers, they shall not overwhelm you; when you walk through fire you shall not be burned, and the flame shall not consume you. For I am the Lord your God, the Holy One of Israel, your Savior" (Isa. 43:1b-3a). There is never an occasion so dismally dark or so seemingly impossible that the Lord God will turn His back upon us and force us to endure it alone. When we live in understanding of divine love we can tighten our arms about Him and also whisper, saying, "It is awfully dark; but I'm not afraid, because my Father is here!" And after saying this confidently we can move ahead knowing the Lord does care and does protect. How much needless care we experience because we lack faith. Faith tells us that we are never really alone.

God's Care

"Oh, My God!"

It was early Wednesday morning, June 6th, 1968, after a "Victory Speech," when several shots were fired from a 22-caliber handgun. Senator Robert F. Kennedy, aspirant for the Democratic

Party's nomination for the presidency, fell mortally wounded. In the midst of the confusion, consternation, and cursing, an unknown voice was heard. "Oh, my God!" were the words.

"Oh, my God!" Even before it was fully known and understood as to what had happened the involuntary and intuitive cry came from the mouth (and heart, we would presume) of one who at that moment spoke for humanity. Tragedy, sorrow, and disaster cause man to express his feelings to the Almighty. Persons not normally given to prayer feel the impulse of turning to God. Man recognizes his personal inadequacies.

The Lord has issued a wonderful invitation, in which He says, "Call upon me in the day of trouble, and I will deliver thee and thou shalt glorify me," but He has also said we are to "pray without ceasing." Lives lived in a correct relationship with Him will be actively engaged in a life of prayer. And certainly this means more than pious mouthings of certain traditional "holy" phrases. In all life's moments—good and bad—that one who is more than just casually acquainted with the Creator-Redeemer will live by attitudes and actions a life that dignifies God's hopes and desires for the highest of His creation.

"Oh, my God!" is an admission of futility and failure. "Oh, my God!" is the expression of the need every man has for an understanding and personal God who will shelter and protect him, not just from transient and physical dangers, but from the spiritual and permanent dangers of all that would destroy the meaning of true living with the ultimate hope in the future. "Oh, my God!" is the helpless wail of this helpless world. Prayer is all these things when spoken from the heart. But from the heart they must be spoken.

Too often man acts as though he can carry on by himself, that somehow or another it is a mark of weakness to call on God for help, strength, and guidance. A clergyman was visiting one of his parishioners who had been confined for several weeks. As he was about to leave he asked if he should offer prayer. "Oh, I guess you needn't bother," said the patient. "I don't think I'm *that* sick." Just see the hatred in the world. We *are* sick! "Oh, my God!"

". . . their soul is melted because of trouble. They reel to and fro, and stagger like a drunken man, and are at their wit's end. Then they cry unto the Lord in their trouble, and he bringeth them out of their distresses. He maketh the storm a calm, so that the waves thereof are still. Then they are glad because they be quiet; so he bringeth them unto their desired haven" (Ps. 107:26-30 KJV).

You Are Never Too Old

Some time ago, a secular newspaper told the story of a little fellow who had reached the epoch in a boy's life when he gets his first pair of "pants like daddy's." The new "grown-up" look unsettled his spiritual equilibrium. Before the occasion of new pants he had been a devout little Christian and joined his little sister every morning in asking the Lord's help and blessing for the day. But this morning, when he looked at his new pants, and felt himself a man, he stopped his little sister as she began to pray as usual, "Lord Jesus, take care of Freddie today, and keep him from harm," and, like poor Simon Peter, in his self-sufficiency, he cried out, "No, Jennie; don't say that; Freddie can take care of himself now." Little Jennie was shocked and frightened, but did not know what to do; and so the day began. Before noon they both climbed up into a cherry tree, and while reaching out for the tempting fruit Freddie went head foremost down into an angle between the tree and the fence. With all his desperate struggles and those of his frightened sister, he was utterly unable to extricate himself. At last he said to Jennie, with a look of mingled shame and intelligence, "Jennie, pray: Freddie can't take care of himself after all." Just then a strong man was coming along the road, and the answer to their prayer came quickly as he took down the fence and freed Freddie. The boy went away from the scene with a lesson for life, to walk like Peter, with bent head and humble trust in a strength and care more mighty than his own.

Simon Peter learned his lesson well, and he remembered what had happened when he thought he was able to "go it alone." One of his sage pieces of advice was this statement: "Humble yourselves therefore under the mighty hand of God, that in due time he may exalt you. Cast all your anxieties on him, for he cares about you" (I Peter 5:6-7). As we live each day we should recognize the need for that One who can and does care about us. There are so many uncertainties and dangers to face each day of our lives that unless we can be comforted with the knowledge that God does care we are prone to become distraught and worried to the point of helpless hopelessness. No matter how old one becomes, he is never too old to need that power which is able to overcome all cares—the power of the living God!

It's the Man on the Cross

An expert swimmer taught college men how to swim and dive. One night he couldn't sleep. He decided to go to the swimming pool and have a swim, hoping that the exercise would induce sleep. He said, "I didn't put the lights on. I knew every inch of the place, and the roof was made of glass. The moon shone through, throwing the shadow of my body on the wall at the other end of the pool. I started to dive. My body and arms made a perfect sign of the cross! I cannot explain why I did not dive at that moment. I had no premonition of danger of any kind. As I stood looking at the shadow of the cross, I began to think of the cross of Christ and its meaning. I was not a Christian. I found myself repeating the words of a hymn I had learned as a boy: 'He died that I might be forgiven.' I cannot tell you how long I stood poised on the diving board, or why I did not dive. I came down from the diving board and walked along the pool to the steps that I knew led to the bottom of the pool and began to descend. I reached the bottom and my feet touched the cold, smooth bottom of the pool! The night before the caretaker had drained the pool dry and I knew nothing about it. I realized then that had I dived, I would have dived to my death! The cross on the wall saved me that night. I was so thankful to God for His mercy in sparing my life I knelt on the cold bricks and asked the Christ of the cross to save my soul. I experienced a twofold deliverance that night!"

What an experience! And what a remarkable insight into the fact that the cross, a symbol of total sacrifice, is worthless if the Man of the cross is not remembered and considered. So often there is a great sentimentality shown for the symbol while the Son of God, the Savior of the world, is shunted into the background. "In the cross of Christ I glory" is sung with gusto, and it does express eternal verities, but we must be very careful to give the one Man the honor and worship due Him. In John 3:16 we read, "For God so loved the world that he gave his only Son, that whoever believes in him should not perish but have eternal life." It's the Man on the cross that counts. The cross, as the wonderful symbol of God's grace, is the instrument that was used. So, as we remember the Lord's sufferings and death, and the cross, let us never forget who He was, and is, and what He has done for us. Yes, "it's the Man on the cross" that counts.

That's All I Want

A mother said to her minister one day as he was making a pastoral call on her, "Will you read this letter? It's from Bob." The kindly pastor sat down and read the letter that seemed to make such an impression on the lady of the house. When he had gotten halfway through he knew why she had wanted him to read it. Bob, her son, was away in the service. This is what he had written: "You know I have a feeling that I am coming home all right. I don't know why, but I feel that God is taking care of that. What I want to say is: When I do get home, I hope that, when we have finished dinner at night and we're all there at the table, we will just stay there and look at one another and realize for just a little while nothing else but the fact that we are there together. That's all I want."

What a wonderful attitude to have insofar as family relationship is concerned. ". . . the fact that we are there together!" Even more wonderful than such a warmth, on the human level, is that which each Christian enjoys and will enjoy everlastingly within the household of the faithful. Jesus has said, "I will come again and will take you to myself, that where I am you may be also" (John 14:3b). We too know that we will be coming home some day. *When* the Lord will call only He knows, but when He does there will be fulfillment of the divine promises. Warmth, joy, fellowship, understanding, and the peace that passes all understanding will be shared by those who trusted in the Lord in this human lifetime and who felt that His time was always their time.

Sometimes we forget the meaning of the term "home." Too often our minds conjure up the idea of a fashionable house in a prestigious neighborhood surrounded by important people. The story is told of a little girl who lived with her folks in cramped quarters in a rather dingy hotel because of the housing shortage near the military base where the father was stationed. A friend said to the man's six-year-old daughter, "Isn't it too bad that you don't have a home?" "Oh, we have a home," the youngster replied quickly, "we just don't have a house to put it in."

No matter what physical conditions we may find ourselves in, we can rest assured that we always have a home. It may be difficult to find a "house" to put it in, but the good Lord has assured us of His loving care and kindness. Think of the joy of just knowing we are there together.

41

They Saw the Light

One black stormy night in the combat zone of the southwest Pacific, United States Air Force pilots were out to intercept an enemy warship fleet. Six very close friends were in that flight, and at dusk had completed their mission. All were safe, but it was dark, hazy, and raining, and they were two hundred miles out at sea, away from their home base, with no beam or homing device to "ride in." Their compasses were not accurate, and they did not know their exact position. Those on the ground were listening to them over the radio. As the time approached for them to arrive, the ground force turned on some searchlights pointing straight up, hoping the pilots could see them.

Time came for them to be near the base and not an engine could be heard and not a wing light could be seen. Over the radio the men on the ground could hear: Dick to Jim, "Do you know where we are?" "Pull up, Pete; you're getting too low." "Can you see the field lights anywhere?" "We should be there. Let's start flying in a big circle." "How much gas have you got?" After a few minutes of silence, and with the tension getting greater and greater by the minute, there came over the radio in a clear, relieved, and happy voice: "I see the light! We're saved! I see the light!" A sigh of relief came from the lips of those who had been alarmed and who were waiting hopefully for the returning flyers. Prayers had been answered. They had seen the light and followed it home to the base safely.

People are still "flying" through an earthly existence "in the dark" and are groping for the meaning to life. Lost in a maze of conflicting teachings and philosophies, one is unable to clearly "see" the pattern before him. And yet the individual is not left to himself, to guide himself to a "safe landing." The great Son of God said, while walking on this earth, ". . . I am the light of the world; he who follows me will not walk in darkness, but will have the light of life" (John 8:12).

Those who have come to the knowledge of God's loving concern for them, in Christ Jesus, do travel in lighted areas. The hand of God directs, leads, and strengthens each one who only looks for that light that shines and dispels the darkness of uncertainty and fear. Have you seen the light and do you follow it confidently?

This Thing Called Love

Twenty years of childless marriage. The couple was not even able to adopt a child to give expression to parental love and care. Then, almost as a miracle, it was discovered the wife was able and going to have a child.

Thrilled, and living in joyful expectation for the day of the birth of their first-born, they thanked God for His kindness. Imagine the sorrow of the doctor and the father when they realized the child was malformed, one arm was missing; there was but a twisted stump of flesh. The father determined to tell his wife the tragic news. Entering into the hospital room at the same time the nurse brought the infant, he noticed the mother proudly looking at the face of the baby. "Perfect, isn't she?" she said as she stroked the child's features. Something in the eyes of her husband warned her all was not well. Slowly she removed the blanket and noticed the disfigurement. She stared, turned her face to the wall in silence, and after a few seconds, again turned her face to her husband and said softly and slowly, "John, the Lord knew just where to send this baby, didn't He? He understood how much we needed her and how much she needs us."

What an example of human love expressed by a mother! What a tribute to mothers everywhere! Remember, though, how much greater is the divine love of God in Christ. Looking at a completely crippled humanity, separated from Him by sin, rebellious and hate-filled, He recognized and recognizes our need for Him. In infinite compassion and love He entered into this world's scene and lifted us to spiritual restoration through the cross and open tomb. Yes, "God so loved the world that he gave his only begotten Son . . ." (John 3:16). Here we have the complete meaning to this thing we call love.

Love, to be meaningful, demands a response. And the only response to love that is worthwhile is love. As a thankful and appreciative child shows consideration, kindness, and love to his parents for all that has been given and shown to him in his helpless period of life, so should we express our love to God who continually cares for us all the days of our lives. This response, on our part, is shown by loyalty to Him and His cause on earth —following His loving example and speaking out against the injustices and hatred shown by godless men, and by proclaiming Him as the only hope of the world. Thank God for mothers but also thank God for God and for this thing called love that has true and lasting meaning.

"Hey, Mister, Wait!"

A well-dressed man was walking slowly down one of the main streets of the city, gazing into the various store window displays. He came to one window that showed a dismal Good Friday scene of the place where the "Man of Galilee" had been slain. Three stark crosses were set in the middle of a greyish-black sky. Disconsolate men and women seemed to be attempting to withdraw into the background. The figure on the center cross, tragic and lifeless, brought an emotional tear to the viewer's eyes.

Suddenly a little boy, of perhaps seven or eight years of age, spoke to the gentleman. "Do you know what that is all about, mister?" he asked. "No, tell me," the man replied. The child, with direct simplicity, recounted the story of the crucifixion of the Lord, including the details of His false arrest, cruel treatment, and death. The man nodded agreement and continued down the street. He had only gone a few yards when he heard the youngster running after him. He stopped and waited. Breathlessly the boy blurted out, "Hey, mister, wait, He rose on Sunday, He's alive!"

We are reliving the experiences of that first "Holy Week" again in our minds. Those who have come to know the factual story of the life of Christ eagerly long for Easter. The sky seems heavy with despondent and dismal disappointment. Dreams are shattered as we think of the wrath of both heaven and hell thrown against Sinless God. All that is holy and meaningful seems to have perished. "Good Friday" becomes "Black Friday." But—"Hey, mister, wait!"

The story has not ended. Easter, with its message of resurrection, is just around the corner. He is alive! Death did not hold Him captive! Satan did not overpower Him! The Lenten season is nearly over. The review of His suffering for us is nearing an end. The resurrection is an attested fact! The four Gospels all ring out with the Good News.

Don't walk away from Calvary's scene despondent. He arose! He's alive!! "Hey, mister, wait!"

Does It Hurt?

A little girl, by the name of Beverly Smith, born in Akron Ohio, almost never cried from the day she entered into the world; she never cried when she bumped her head; she didn't even cry when she burned her hand on a hot stove. The only time she really showed any emotion and gave vent to tears was when she was either hungry or angry. The doctors soon discovered that she had a defect in the central nervous system for which there is no known cure. The medical men told the parents she must be watched constantly; the child might break a bone and continue using it until it could not be set properly; she might develop appendicitis without nature's usual warning of pain. Spanking her to make her more careful about hot stoves and knives would do no good; she wouldn't feel it. Life without pain would be perpetually dangerous to her. Only alert and careful supervision and love was the answer.

This true account of a life without physical feeling can serve as an application to the spiritual life of people. Often one wonders why there is so much suffering in the lives of those who profess and live the Christian life. Many times the follower of the Christ of Calvary is bewildered and confused over the fact he must bear pain, disappointment, and frustrating experiences. The Lord does send troubles to His own but He has a purpose. "For the Lord disciplines him whom He loves, and chastises every son whom he receives. . . . If you are left without discipline, in which all have participated, then you are illegitimate children and not sons." (Heb. 12:6, 8). The "hurts" and the "harms" that enter into lives serve as warnings against the bigger "hurts" of life just as warnings given by our nervous systems keep us away from fire and other hurts.

The "alive" Christian will constantly examine himself to see whether he has become so accustomed to the sinfulness of this world that he has become insensible to the presence of sin. The Book of Proverbs tells us, "Whom the Lord loveth he correcteth" (3:12). Certainly one should be thankful that the Lord cares enough to keep one sensible to the "hurt" of sin. Let each one ask himself this question as he sees God's way violated: "Does it hurt?"

Opportunity Through Affliction

A story is told of a Christian girl in India, who was about to be married. She was attractive, and one of the most capable girls in the institution. But sores appeared on her hands, and it was discovered that she had leprosy. She was removed from the orphanage and sent to the leper asylum. She was dressed in her beautiful white flowing garments as she walked with her brother into that awful place. The women who were there were dirty and filthy, and their faces looked sad and hopeless. When she saw them, she threw her head on her brother's shoulder, and wept and sobbed, "My God," she said, "am I going to become as they are?" She was so distressed, that those about her were afraid she might jump into the well. The missionaries sympathized with her, and asked her if she wouldn't like to be a help to those poor women. A ray of hope came to her and she caught the vision. She started a school, and taught the women to sing, read, and write. She could play, so the missionaries bought her a folding organ. The houses were made clean, neat, and tidy; the women washed their clothes and combed their hair; and that horrible place became a place of blessing.

After being there for some time, she said, "When I first came to the asylum I doubted that there was a God. Now I know that God had a work for me to do, and if I had not become a leper, I never would have discovered my work. Every day I live, I thank Him for having sent me here, and that He has given me this work to do."

Sometimes when affliction strikes, one is prone to sit back and bemoan his sorrowful fate. Forgetting (especially for the Christian) that God can use all forms of tribulation, tragedy, and testing for His own good purposes, the afflicted individual loses all incentive and desire to move forward. Paul, writing to the Romans, once said, "Rejoice in your hope, be patient in tribulation, be constant in prayer. Contribute to the needs of the saints, practice hospitality" (12:12-13). There is always something that can be done regardless of the seeming darkness of the day. With the understanding that God knows the situation and is able to transform the apparent misfortune into a blessing, the afflicted person will seek the door that leads to a fuller and happier life for himself and others. If we trust God to lead us, we will find there is opportunity through affliction.

"Wait Until I'm Finished"

One day a small boy was attracted to the kitchen of his home by the sound of an egg beater in operation. Entering the room he saw his mother preparing to bake a cake. All the ingredients were on the table, eggs, sugar, chocolate, sour milk, baking soda, flour, all the necessary ingredients. Seeing a small crumb of the chocolate lying aside he quickly picked it up and placed it in his mouth—and discovered the bitterness of it! "Surely mother will not use anything *so* bitter," he thought to himself. Seeing the sour milk he asked, "Mother, are you going to mix the bitter chocolate with sour milk?" Her answer was, "Wait until I'm finished." With his nose turned up the boy left the room thinking, "What kind of a good tasting cake can mother make out of those ingredients that taste so bitter and look so unappetizing?" However, that evening, after the main portion of the meal had been eaten mother went into the kitchen and came back with a delicious chocolate cake the boy loved so much. "Try the cake, son," said the mother. With some hesitation and doubt the boy ate a small piece, then a larger one, and finally began eating with great delight. It was good! It was just as mother had promised, but it was necessary to heed her advice when she had said, "Wait until I'm finished."

In Romans 8:28 we read, "We know that in everything God works for good with those who love him, who are called according to his purpose." Too often we are ready to make judgment against the so-called misfortunes of life when they fall on us. We become like the small boy in the kitchen who wants to turn away from the cake ingredients because they do not taste good in their separated state. We forget that life is made up of various conditions, sad and joyful, sweet and bitter, disappointing and fulfilling. We are not willing to have God tell us to "Wait until I'm finished."

If we believe that God is the God of history who not only enters history but makes history, and if we believe that He is a God of love who desires only good for those who are His, then we can have faith that says through the "raw" ingredients of experiences, sad as well as joyful, our "finished" lives will be good, wholesome, and enjoyable. He does love us. Christ's life and activity proves it. But we must wait for the finished product. Don't make a snap judgment. Listen and believe when He says, "Wait until I'm finished."

May We Substitute?

Years ago, before large shopping complexes became common, a man lived in a town where he could never buy anything to fit him. Occasionally he sent away to a certain large store for what he needed, and they would send him printed order forms. At the bottom of the forms were some such words as these: "If we have not the article you ordered in stock, may we substitute?" Once he said, "Yes," and they wrote, "We are sorry we have not the article in stock that you ordered, but we are substituting-------- in its place," and they sent him something that was worth double the price he paid for the original piece of merchandise. The store from which the article had been purchased had made it a rule, if they could not supply the article originally ordered, to substitute with one of a much better quality. After the initial experience, the man printed boldly so they would understand it—"Y-E-S" on every order that he sent. He knew that he would not be "short-changed" or come out worse. He relied on the honesty and the good will policy of the store.

Isn't this the attitude the Christian should have as he approaches God in prayer? So many times prayers are directed as "demands" with the implication being, "If you can't give me what I want just don't send anything." Man is unwilling to take God at His word. The individual does not believe that God's desire to substitute, when necessary in His wisdom, is only for the good of man and will be of much better quality than the original request. Someone has rightly said, "Thank God we do not always get those things for which we pray."

In the Letter of James we read, "Every good endowment and every perfect gift is from above, coming down from the Father of lights with whom there is no variation or shadow due to change" (1:17). That which is "good" and "perfect" must be for our benefit. Yet time after time the finite mind would fault and question the infinite mind of God. Because of shortsightedness or purely personal desires, we sometimes ask for immediate "benefits," whatever the word "benefits" may mean to us. We forget that only God knows the future and what is truly good for us. As the poet once said:

>My life is but a weaving
>Between my Lord and me;

I cannot choose the colors
Nor all the pattern see.
Sometimes He chooseth sorrow,
And I in foolish pride
Forget He sees the upper
And I the under side.

As we make our requests to Him in prayer let us say "Y-E-S" to His substitutions.

Home

Parental Responsibility

One beautiful Sunday morning a father took his little child out into the fields to see the wonderful scenery that nature provides. Since it was a hot day, he lay down under a shady tree and decided to rest as his child ran in circles in the area where they were. The little child began to gather wild flowers and little blades of grass and always returned to where father was resting, saying: "Pretty, pretty!" At last, the weather being mild and sunshiny, father fell fast asleep, and while he was sleeping, the child wandered farther away from the spot. When he awoke, his first thought was: "Where is my child?"

He looked all around, but he could not see his beloved one. He shouted at the top of his voice, but all he heard was the echo. Running to a little hill, he looked around and shouted again. No response! Then going to a precipice at some distance, he looked down, and there, upon the rocks and briars, he saw the mangled form of the child he loved so well. He rushed to the spot, took up the lifeless corpse, and hugged it to his chest, and accused himself of being the murderer of his child. While he was sleeping his child had wandered over the precipice.

What a picture this is of the parents of our present generation. Sleeping "at the switch" they allow their children to engage in dangerous practices. Not having guidance and direction, there are many who fall over the "precipice" of permissiveness and folly. There is no sane head to advise and direct. There is no danger signal that can be heard, because the "father is fast asleep."

The Book of Proverbs states: "For the Lord reproves him whom he loves, as a father the son in whom he delights." Just as the Lord

God desires only the best for his own, so the earthly father desires that which is "best" for his own. In a day and age where permissiveness seems to be a way of life, the sincere and concerned father will be alert to the dangers that face those offspring who are precious in his sight. There can be no "mild and sunshiny weather" that will lull one into "sleepiness." There are so many dangers to the life and soul of the individual that the Christian parent will be aware of the spirit of the world that will bring his child to the "precipice."

The Word of God presents insights that only God can provide. The will of God is clearly revealed in His Holy Book—the Bible. Parents who truly love their children will diligently lead the way by example and words of caution and advice. How about it? Are we willing to assume "parental responsibility"?

Home

What Kind of Home Do You Have?

Christian parents must set a good example for their children by putting their faith into practice. The truth of this statement is illustrated in a story about a boy called "Junior." When he was fourteen, his father came home wearing a happy grin, and said, "Got pinched for speeding, but Jake down at the city hall got the ticket fixed for me." A year later the lad was with his mother when she backed the family car into a tree. "We'll say someone ran into us when we were parked downtown," she said. "So we can collect insurance for it." At the age of sixteen he listened to his grandfather reminiscing about the "good old days of rationing" when he made $100,000 black-marketing cars. That same night Uncle John bragged that on a good share of his business he sent no bills and took no checks because he wasn't going to be "a sucker and let those punks in the Internal Revenue Department get all my money." When Junior turned eighteen, his family pulled every possible string to get him a paid scholarship at an Ivy League school, even lying about the family income to obtain financial aid. The young man had a rough time scholastically, however, and bought the answers to a calculus exam from an upperclassman. He was caught and expelled. When he returned home, his mother burst into weeping, and cried, "How could you have done this to us? This isn't the way we raised you!" But wasn't he only carrying out the lessons he had learned from the adults who had helped shape his early life? They had lived a lie, and Junior followed their example. Never forget that children are greatly influenced by the lives of their parents. The examples of father and mother will make a deeper imprint upon the young than physical punishment, admonition, or instruction.

How different the above story to the one that tells about a message from a son to his mother on Mother's Day. The letter came to a certain lady, from her son, who was serving in South Vietnam, and it is a highly treasured one. In the letter, Allen Brafman, wrote to his mother, Mrs. George Brafman, of Floral Park, New York: "Well, here it is your day and I'm over here so far away. But I want you to know that all through my life I have appreciated everything you have done for me." Allen, twenty years old, had enlisted in the Air Force almost three years before, just after completing high school. For the last nine months he had been stationed with the Air Police at DaNang, in South Vietnam. "By coming over here," he continued, "I hope I'll make you almost as proud of me as I know a college diploma would have." He concluded, "Maybe you'll get to see my diploma yet . . . anyway, have a wonderful Mother's Day."

Honesty

The Price Is Too Great

In a certain bank there was a trust department in which four young men and one older man were employed. It was decided by the directors that they would promote the older employee and also promote one of the younger men to have charge of the trust department after the older gentleman was removed to his new position. After considering the merits of each of the men, one of the four younger men was selected for the new position and to receive a substantial increase in salary. It was decided to notify him of the promotion that afternoon at four o'clock. At the noon hour the young man went to a cafeteria for lunch. One of the directors was behind him in the line with several other customers in between them. The director saw the young man select his food including a small piece of butter. The butter, he flipped on his plate, and threw some food on top of it to hide it from the cashier. In this way he lied to the cashier about what was on his plate. That afternoon the directors met to notify the young man that they had intended giving him the promotion, but that because of what had been seen in the cafeteria, they must discharge him. They felt that they could not have as the head of their trust department one who would lie and steal.

Paul, writing to the Corinthian people said, "For we aim at what is honorable not only in the Lord's sight but also in the sight of men" (II Cor. 8:21). Even the world has the axiom, "Honesty is the best policy." Yet there are many people in the world today who will attempt to take advantage of situations and gain for themselves free "a small piece of butter." But one who knows, feels, and understands the righteousness of God will not deliberately determine to defraud another. No matter how slight the deed, it is still a transgression of divine law. It is only a matter of degree.

Certainly it should never be felt that endangering one's reputation for any amount is worth the effort. When one in any manner or shape attempts to unlawfully gain for himself an advantage by "stealing" (whether it be by misrepresentation or lie), he subjects himself to the position of the untrustworthy and unreliable. Perhaps those in positions of government, from a federal status to the local level, should be reminded of this fact: "The price is too great to pay!"

Humility

"I'm a Captain"

A young man who had been brought up in one of the worst slums of New York, rose to fame and fortune in the theatrical field through his literary talents. He bought a yacht, and although he hired a man to run it for him, he himself assumed the title of "Captain." He got himself a uniform with all the gold braid and brass buttons he could find. Outfitted in this fashion, he invited his old mother to go for a cruise. Mother had come to the United States from eastern Europe, and she had retained the native common sense that so many immigrants have. Humility, to her, was a virtue. The boat had been moved from the dock, out into open water, and the young man went below to change into the uniform that he wore so proudly. A few moments later he came out on deck to parade before his mother. "Look, Momma," he said, "I'm a captain." The wise old lady surveyed him calmly and then, as one accustomed to deflating the ego of a conceited child, she softly answered, "Sammy, by you, you is a captain, by me you is a captain, but by captains you is no captain."

There are many people who need to realize their own importance. According to one's own standards he may be a "good" man; by all outward appearances his life may be considered "good." But what about the standard that God sets? Is there one single person who can claim the perfect goodness found only in Christ? Can one, without the direction, leading, and strengthening of the Spirit, solidly and confidently say, "I'm a captain"?

The Word of God, the Bible, says that according to divine holiness and perfection there is no such thing as human goodness and that ". . . all our righteousnesses are as filthy rags" (Isa. 64:6). This is a sobering fact. This is a "put down" of human life lived without the understanding of the need for a complete holy coverage, made possible by the knowledge and understanding of the grace of God, found in Jesus Christ alone. No matter how one tries by himself, he cannot wear "captain's" clothes. Actions and attitudes give cruel proof that outward appearance is not enough. Just as, because of lack of experience on the part of the captain, the boat would flounder and sink, so does a human life lose direction when lived without the leadership of the only qualified One, Jesus Christ. Let us not fool ourselves with human philosophies and changing moralities and suit ourselves up in the glitter of the world's imperfect thought and conceitedly say, "Look, I'm a captain."

Humility

"Where Is Humility?"

A rider on horseback, many years ago, came across a squad of soldiers who were trying to move a heavy piece of timber. A corporal stood by, giving lordly orders to "heave." But the piece of timber was a trifle too heavy for the squad. "Why don't you help them?" asked the quiet man on the horse, addressing the important corporal. "Me? Why, I'm a corporal, sir!" Dismounting, the stranger carefully took his place with the soldiers. "Now, all together, boys—heave!" he said. And the big piece of timber slid into place. The stranger mounted his horse and addressed the corporal. "The next time you have a piece of timber for your men to handle, corporal, send for the commander-in-chief." The horseman was George Washington.

Perhaps one of the lost virtues of men today is that of humility. So often each one thinks so highly of himself that many of the tasks in life that could be accomplished by cooperation are left undone because it is "beneath my dignity." Scripture says, "Humble yourselves therefore under the mighty hand of God, that in due time he may exalt you" (I Peter 5:6). A humble person is an asset, wherever he may be.

It would appear that the "higher" one ascends in our society the more the need for humility. The people of the United States have selected and elected a new president. Undoubtedly, many of the top Cabinet posts will go to "new" men. Under the pressures of today's living it is vital these men understand the problems they face and the tremendous responsibilities that have been laid upon them. Truly a humble spirit should prevail within them. None of them should have such an exaggerated sense of self-importance that would cause them to remain aloof from any task. The prayers of loyal citizens, regardless of party politics, must ascend to the throne of grace in their behalf, and among the petitions should be that which asks and begs, "Lord, keep our leaders humble."

Humility should be a part of each Christian's life, regardless of station. Each one is recognize himself as he is. Those who have greater talents are to thank God for them and ask that the talents be used beneficially for others and that they be used in an honest humility. Those who stand in positions of honor and trust, whether in the home, in community affairs, national or international situations, whether prominent in the public eye or lost in the obscurity of the "trivial" should desire to serve in humility so that, pleasing God, they may be exalted by Him. "Humble yourselves in the sight of the Lord, and he shall lift you up" (James 4:10 KJV). "Whosoever shall exalt himself shall be abased; and he that shall humble himself shall be exalted" (Matt. 24:12).

How Easy to Forget

The story is old, but it bears repeating. Two men were walking toward each other on a street of one of our larger cities. As they neared each other, the one man recognized the other as a friend and acquaintance of a good many years. However, the other man gave no sign that he recognized the other. The first man stopped his friend, Joe, and said to him: "Joe, don't tell me you were going to pass by without even saying hello? Don't you know me?" "Oh, yes," said Joe, "I recognized you, but there was no reason for me to stop and chat with you. After all, we don't have very much in common anymore. Why don't you just keep going your way, and I'll go mine!"

"But Joe," said the first man again, "why should you feel this way? Wasn't I the one who made it possible for you to get a job after you had been fired, and didn't I loan you sufficient money for your child's operation when you were broke? Don't you remember the time I took time from my busy schedule to talk to your wife when she was about to sue you for divorce? And remember just last month when I assured your present employer that you are a capable man and should be considered for a promotion? Have you forgotten all these things? Why do you say that we have nothing in common, anymore?" Looking him straight in the eye, the second man replied very tersely, Oh, yes, everything you have said is true. You did get me a job after I had been fired; you loaned me money for my child's operation; you took time to talk to Mabel, my wife, and persuade her not to divorce me, and you did recommend me for the promotion I received last month. But what have you done for me recently?"

"What a thankless person," we might exclaim, that after all the consideration and concern shown, someone should take such an attitude. Yet is it not true that many a person, knowingly or unknowingly, acts the same way to God? The Giver of every good and perfect gift is many times ignored because humans so easily forget and say, in effect, "What have you done for me recently?" The psalmist says, "Bless the Lord, O my soul; and all that is within me, bless his holy name. Bless the Lord, O my soul, and forget not all his benefits" (Ps. 103:1-2). All that we have, are, hope to be in Christ, comes from Him. How do you feel? Is it easy to forget?

From Advocate to Judge

When he was a young man, Judge Warren Candler practiced law. One of his clients was charged with murder. The young lawyer went all-out in his effort to clear his client of the charge. There were some extenuating circumstances, and the lawyer made the most of them in his plea before the jury. Too, there were present in the court the aged father and mother of the man charged with murder. The young lawyer wrought greatly on the sympathies and emotions of the jury by frequent references to the God-fearing parents. In due course the jury retired for deliberation. After reaching a verdict, they returned to the jury box. Their verdict read, "We find the defendant not guilty!" The young lawyer, himself a Christian, had a serious talk with his cleared client. He warned him to steer clear of evil ways, and trust God's power to keep him straight.

Years passed. The man was again arraigned. Again the charge was murder. The lawyer who had defended him at his first trial was now the judge on the bench. At the conclusion of the trial the jury rendered its verdict: "Guilty!" Ordering the condemned man to stand for sentence, Judge Candler said, "At your first trial I was your lawyer, your advocate. Today I am your judge. The verdict of the jury makes it mandatory for me to sentence you to be hanged by the neck until you are dead. May God be merciful to your soul!"

The Christian truly believes that Jesus Christ came into the world to redeem the world—to save it from itself. His entire lifetime was spent in bringing the good news of reconciliation through His substitutionary life. However, it is plainly revealed that the time will come when the period of opportunity will end, when man will have had his chance to be called a child of God. At that time, as the psalmist says, "He comes to rule the earth. He will judge the world with righteousness, and the peoples with equity" (Ps. 98:9). All that He effectively accomplished with His life will point out the guilt of those who have rejected Him. No longer will they see the great and loving Savior as the One who is standing as the Advocate. Rather, they will behold Him as the righteous Judge who will be forced to pronounce the verdict, "Guilty!" Now, we can have Him as our Advocate—as one who pleads our case. Now is the time to prepare ourselves so we may hear Him, as Judge, say, "Not guilty, you are free in Me!"

"He Dared Not Face the Music"

Years ago, in Old China, lived a man who was a member of the emperor's orchestra, although he could not play a note. He had obtained his position as a flute player in the royal band by influence, and for many years, whenever the musicians played, he sat with them and held his flute against his lips, pretending to play the plaintive airs and love songs of his native land. But he never dared to blow even softly into the instrument for fear he would cause a discord and be unmasked. For this performance he received a modest salary and managed to live comfortably. But there came a day when it was the emperor's wish and whim to have each of his musicians play alone. The flutist was dismayed, and as the day approached he became desperate. For a time he took lessons from a professional, but to no avail; he had no musical ear and no talent for the flute. Then he pretended to be ill, but was afraid he would be betrayed by the royal physician, who was sent to attend him. On the morning of his solo appearance, he took poison and died rather than face the music. This, then, is the origin of an old Chinese phrase, "He dared not face the music."

There are many people in the world today who claim the title "Christian" who also are living a lie. Although professing to be followers of that One who entered in the world's scene as Savior and Redeemer, they neither have the attitude nor the action of one of the Christ-men that is expected of him. The Lord was much aware of a situation such as this arising for He said one time, "Not everyone who says to me, 'Lord, Lord,' shall enter the kingdom of heaven, but he who does the will of my Father who is in heaven" (Matt. 7:21). When one notices that many who feel their responsibilities toward God and man are fulfilled by following certain liturgical patterns, rites, and ceremonies but have no compassion toward their fellowmen who stand in need of care and concern; when one notices the "people of God" become self-centered, interested in only their own causes and ignoring the injustices perpetrated on minorities; he is forced to wonder if there are not many, many people who are like the Chinese flutist! Some day each one will be forced to "face the music" of judgment. Looking ahead to that day, who will be able to face it before the one and Living God?

What Do You Defend?

There are many stories told about Abraham Lincoln and his views on morality and the way a Christian should live. One of these stories concerns itself about a man who came to his law office to secure his services. The man was asked by Lincoln to state his case. After he had spoken to the great humanitarian, he was told by Lincoln, "I cannot serve you, for you are wrong, and the other party is right." The man who was endeavoring to secure the services of the young lawyer, answered, "That is none of your business if I hire and pay you for taking the case." Lincoln's answer to that statement was, "Not my business! My business is never to defend wrong. I never take a case that is manifestly wrong." The man who was attempting to hire Lincoln replied, "Not for any amount of pay?" Lincoln's answer was, "Not for all you are worth."

How far in a utilitarian direction we have apparently traveled in our present day and age! There seems to be so little thought given to what is right or wrong in the sight of God and/or man. The Book of Proverbs in the Old Testament says, "Every way of a man is right in his own eyes, but the Lord weighs the heart" (21:2). What then is the criterion one uses to defend the "right"?

We are living in an age that seems to reflect the desire of people to find reward for themselves, regardless of what is "right or wrong." The terms "right" and "wrong" only mean something if they enhance a situation whereby the individual is benefited. And yet we are to understand that it only measures up to meaningfulness if it can be measured in the sight of the Lord. It is the Lord who "weighs the heart."

We are forced to ask the question, "What do I defend?" "What is it that makes me act the way I do and causes me to respond to varied situations?" Can I honestly say that I am truly interested in those about me, or am I only interested in my personal welfare and that which will aid and enlarge my personal living? Here again the Lord God, looking into the depths of our hearts, has the honest answer. It takes extreme courage to stand against what is considered "popular."

Continuing in the Book of Proverbs, we read, "To do righteousness and justice is more acceptable to the Lord than sacrifice"

(21:3). On what basis do we make decisions and fight for what we believe is right? Is it God's will or man's? Just what is it we defend?

The Way of the Cross

Pittsburgh's airport is one of the biggest and best-equipped in the nation. Two seconds in flying time from the airport and in direct line with one of its busiest runways is the steeple of Union Church. "Ever since the terminal opened," said the pastor, William R. Ruschaput, "planes have buzzed the belfry like bees after honey. It got so bad that low-flying jets turned our Sunday evening services into sudden prayer meetings." Reluctant to have their steeple carried away by some careless and unwary pilot, the church topped it with an eight-foot neon-lighted cross. The church is on the highest point near the airport and the lighted cross can be seen at night by planes all the way from the Ohio border. One of the pilots made this interesting comment regarding the lighted cross: "Most of us are using it as a guide to the field."

Henry Francis Lyte penned the words to the familiar hymn, "Abide with Me." The last verse says:

Hold Thou Thy cross before my closing eyes;
Shine through the gloom, and point me to the skies;
Heaven's morning breaks, and earth's vain shadows flee:
In life, in death, O Lord, abide with me.

If it becomes possible for a man-made beacon to lead airplane pilots safely to the man-made runway of an airport constructed by man, how much more sure and certain is it for any and every one to be guided safely to the eternal kingdom of God, through the divinely inspired cross of Calvary? For over nineteen hundred years man has been directed to the fulfillment of forgiveness and pardon that leads to the heavenly "airport." Paul writes, "For in him [Jesus] all the fullness of God was pleased to dwell, and through him to reconcile to himself all things, whether on earth or in heaven, making peace by the blood of his cross" (Col. 1:19-20). Through the darkness of sin the light of the cross shines brightly and constantly. It leads home, as the familiar gospel song says:

I must needs go home by the way of the cross,
There's no other way but this;
I shall ne'er get sight of the Gates of Light,
If the way of the cross I miss.
The way of the cross leads home.

J. B. Pounds

This is the season of Lent. Do you see the light of the cross? Are you following "the way of the cross"?

You Have to Open Your Hand

Some time ago an American tourist landed in Malaya. Upon reaching shore he was met at the dock by a little native boy with a monkey in a cage. "Wanna buy monkey?" the boy asked. "Only one dollar!" Showing no interest in purchasing the little creature the tourist walked toward the hotel. "Seventy-five cents?" cried the boy. Then, "For only fifty cents, mister." "Here is some small change, boy, you can have it and keep the monkey," the man said. The boy was about to leave happily when the American asked him how he had caught the monkey. "Oh, it is easy," replied the boy. "First you find a gourd that has grown to full length. Then you tie a cord around half of it so that half does not swell; the other half continues to swell, and so a narrownecked bottle is formed. I cut the gourd from the vine, hollow it out, drop in a couple handfuls of rice, and tie the gourd to a tree. The monkey smells the rice, puts his paw in to grab it, but cannot pull his paw out. If he would drop the rice, he could get away, but so long as he holds on to the food his paw acts like a cork in reverse; he is a prisoner of his own greed. He chatters, pulls, and tugs, but he holds onto the rice. I slip a bamboo cage around him, then I break the gourd. The monkey eats the rice and is sold down the river."

This is a picture of many people who have their hands full of trouble, difficulties, worries, and anxieties. Peter said, "Cast all your anxieties on him, for he cares about you" (I Peter 5:7). Obstinate, troubled, and without confident faith, man does, at times, come to the Lord with his difficulties, but, like the monkey, although he places his hand in the hand of his Savior he will not open it to drop the cares of the world into the Lord's hand. He is a prisoner of his own weakness and fear. Like the monkey, man is "sold down the river," not by that One who desires that all men be saved, but by his own unwillingness to trust God.

During that period of time known as Lent, many churchgoers take time to review the great cost of salvation. The cross of Calvary, symbolizing the full extent of divine life, is looked at, and the Man of the cross is again seen as the only hope for a sinful world. Would that those who come to Calvary, filled with worries, frustrations, anxieties, and feelings of incapabilities, be willing to open hands and say with the hymnist, "Nothing in my hands I bring. Simply to thy cross I cling." Remember, you have to open your hand.

Living Meaningfully

Life Begins At ?

It seems we are living in an age when youth, and youth alone, is glorified. Everything points to the advantages and the "glamor" of youth. Beauty contests that emphasize the young and glamorous girl; sporting events that point out the vitality of youth; physical activity that can only be found in those who are in the "hey-day" of strength. All these things lead people to believe that age is only important if it is in the realm of the young. Yet think for a moment: Between the ages of seventy and eighty-three Commodore Vanderbilt added about 100 million to his fortune. Kant at seventy-four wrote his *Anthropology, Metaphysics of Ethics and Strife of the Faculties*. Tintoretto at seventy-four painted the vast paradise canvas seventy-four feet by eighty. Verdi at seventy-four produced his masterpiece, *Otello;* at eighty, *Falstaff* and at eighty-five the famous "Ave Maria," "Stabat Mater," and "Te Deum." Lamarck at seventy-eight completed his great zoological work, *The Natural History of the Invertebrates*. Oliver Wendell Holmes at seventy-nine wrote *Over the Teacup*. Cato at eighty began the study of Greek. Goethe at eighty completed *Faust*. Tennyson at eighty-three wrote, "Crossing the Bar." Titian at ninety-eight painted his historic picture of the "Battle of Lepanto."

So what is youth and what is old age? Being creatures of time we too often make judgments on vitality, strength, wisdom, and ability on the basis of age. How old is he? How many years did she work in her last position? What length of time did they experience related problems? In some cases youth is admired and sought. In other cases youth is despised and ignored while "maturity" has advantages. When does life actually begin?

Scripture says that "a thousand years in thy sight are but as yesterday when it is past: and as a watch in the night" (Ps. 90:4). In other words, as far as the Lord God is concerned, life begins when one comes to the realization of who he is in the sight of his Maker and Redeemer. Without the knowledge of his origin and his ultimate goal, man never lives. He may live his allotted three score years, and ten; he may even reach four score years, or more; yet, "is their strength labor and sorrow; for it is soon cut off, and we fly away" (Ps. 90:10 KJV). Now, at the very present time, one can live . . . if he has learned the meaning of life as God has intended it and has guaranteed it in Jesus Christ, the Savior, who gave His life that we might have life and have it abundantly. When a person realizes God's goodness and salvation, then, and only then, does life really begin. Age has nothing to do with it!

Living Meaningfully

A New Name—A New Life

A man once caught another in the very act of picking his pocket. When caught, the would-be pick-pocket and thief excused himself by saying that he was out of work and starving, and how, after he had served a term of imprisonment, nobody would employ him. Whenever he gave his name his reputation became known, and no one would trust him. "Well," said the man whose pocket had been picked, "take my name, which I fortunately never have had recorded on a police record and which is considered good. I give you my name with my blessing. Take it and keep it clean." He then took steps to find the man employment, giving his name to the employer.

Fifteen years later the Good Samaritan was told that a gentleman was waiting in his outer office to see him. A glance at his visitor's card revealed that he bore the same name as himself, and when he opened his lounge door to see his visitor, he was confronted by a man of fine and noble appearance, who said, "I have called to tell you that today I have been made a partner in the firm to which you recommended me fifteen years ago, and all you see me to be, I owe to your noble generosity, and above all to the gift of your name which is still as good as it was when you gave it to me. God bless you, sir, and reward you.''

In much the same manner the Lord God has given us a "new name"—"Christian"—a Christ-man. Paul states very clearly, "Therefore, if any one is in Christ, he is a new creation; the old has passed away, behold the new has come" (II Cor. 5:17). "The old has passed away"—all that separates the natural man from God is set aside, and in the Lord Jesus Christ the new man, with the indwelling Christ, is accepted as God's child. So often the question is raised, "What good is it to be a Christian?" as though the discipline and spirit of the Christlife is a hindrance to the opportunity to express one's full humanity. The truth of the matter is that only in, with, and through Christ can one understand what it is to be human and to act and react as the Creator originally intended man to act. Though born in sin, and therefore separated from a perfect God, through the redemptive power of Jesus one is reestablished. His "good" and perfect name is given to each one who will not reject divine love. His life is considered for man's good, and His relationship to the Almighty becomes man's relationship to God. In Christ one receives a new name—and a new life!

Living Meaningfully

Profit Without Gain

On September 30, 1863, there died in a little town of Alsace, an idiotic beggar woman. She was an object of curiosity to those who knew her strange history. Her one crowning moment of insane excitement came during the French Revolution when the godless mob had elevated her to the "throne" as "Goddess of Reason." Sitting on the altar in the cathedral of Notre Dame, clad in white robes, ornamented with a blue mantle and red cap and holding a pike in her hand, she had mocked the Christ of the Christian Church and was hailed as that one who was to redeem France from all error and distress. Seventy years later, old, blind, idiotic, in want and misery, she left this world she was to have saved!

Popularity and pride—material goods and glory—status and security all pass into the pages of history. All such things are temporary at best. If one has only a materialistic goal in life he will also "pass into the night" disillusioned and in complete despair. "What shall it profit a man if he shall gain the whole world and lose his own soul?"

There is only one lasting gift that can be had. There is only one person who can give that gift. The gift of life, abundant life, life in proper relationship with the God of creation, can be had through that One who came in the form of a human being, true God and true man, born of the virgin Mary some twenty centuries ago, and gave His life as a ransom for many. We know His purpose and the results of His sinless life. We have had given to us, without cost, His goodness. We are reestablished in love to Him who made us and would call us His own. There is so little time! There are so many distractions! There are too many false "rainbows" beckoning to us with the lying promise of the "pot of gold." Gold tarnishes and loses its value and material possessions rot and decay. Only the love of God, in Christ Jesus, the Savior and Redeemer, is lasting.

To have lasting meaning, a life must be in proper relationship with the Divine. This can only take place when one has come to the saving knowledge of all that the Man of Galilee, the "Man for Others," as He has been called, has done in our behalf. The pre-Easter call is for all men to turn to the cross of Calvary and see evidenced the love of God that passes all human understanding. To see more than an example of suffering for a principle but the willingness to sacrifice a sinless life that sinners might be saved. You can't take it with you. All your human profit becomes loss. Only what Christ gives remains as gain!

Love for Others

A City Was Built

An ancient legend tells of two brothers who lived on adjoining farms. One had a large family, while the other had no children. Both farms produced abundant harvests. One brother said, "My brother has no family, all the joy he has is in his possessions. I will slip some of my grain into his field." The other said, "My brother has a large family. I will slip some of my grain into his field." And so they did each night, and each wondered why his harvest was not diminished, until they met one night and knew the secret. And there, the legend goes, they built the city of peace, Jerusalem.

They met at night armed with a gift of love for each other. They could have met with each carrying a gun. There could have been violence. The city of peace would never have been built. It would seem that modern man could learn a lesson from this legend. Why is there such violence? Where has the "bearing of gifts" been lost? Is love and concern for one's fellowman completely eliminated? "Thou shalt love thy neighbor as thyself," says the Lord God. Has the voice of the divine Creator been stilled?

We are amazed and frightened at the cruel and inhumane acts that surround us. Women and children dare not walk the streets of our cities at night. Public figures are the targets of madmen's guns, knives, and bombs. Respect for property and person is seldom shown, even in so-called "decent" neighborhoods. Destruction is the goal in life. What isn't liked or agreed with must go—and go violently. How can cities of peace be built? Is there no hope for bringing into being modern Jerusalems? What is the answer, if there is an answer, to our besetting sin of lovelessness?

The modern sophisticate ridicules "old time religion." Today's society has no time for those principles that guided and directed grandpa and grandma in the "good old days." And yet God cries out, "Be still and know that I am God." His way is the only way. His love must be reflected in the lives of men if there is to be any hope for peace and tranquility.

There is a tremendous need for "cities" to be built. "Cities" of peace, hope, love, concern, understanding, good-will, and consideration. They can be built if each person would be willing to share his good fortune with those of lesser fortune. One cannot make a fist when he shakes hands. Can't we extend our hands and hearts to God through our love for those about us? Let it be said that by our actions a "city" was built.

Love for Others

Everybody Is in a Hurry

Evening rush-hour traffic streamed out of downtown Rochester, New York. On the outskirts of the business district, cars and trucks swung onto four-lane Interstate 490 and picked up speed. It was 5:30 P.M., Tuesday. For most of the motorists, it was the end of another routine day at the office or plant. Then something happened that made that day different from all other days. As the cars bore down on the Route 36 interchange, a little girl suddenly appeared out of the darkness along the shoulder of the road. She was naked, or nearly so, and some witnesses said she was waving as if trying to hail passing cars. They also noticed an auto along the shoulder of the road, backing toward the girl.

Police now believe that what the drivers saw was possibly the last desperate plea for help by Carmen Colon, ten years old, a petite Puerto Rican child who had been abducted from her Rochester neighborhood only an hour before. Somehow, police theorized, she momentarily escaped from her abductor in the car along the shoulder in a frantic break for safety. But, nobody stopped. And two days later, almost at the same hour of the day, Carmen's body was found in a ditch in a remote section two miles away. An autopsy showed she had been violently attacked and strangled. The news item closed with this question: "Why didn't one of the hundreds of motorists who passed the girl by, stop to help her?" Was everyone so anxious to get somewhere that the sight of a little girl in distress made no impression? Yes, everyone is in a hurry! All too many people do not want to get "involved." Consequently there are ever so many people in need of sympathetic action by their fellowman who never feel the concern of society.

In I John 3:17-18, we read these words: "But if anyone has the world's goods and sees his brother in need, yet closes his heart against him, how does God's love abide in him? Little children, let us not love in word or speech but in deed and in truth." "Love—in deed and in truth!" Because of the ongoing "warfare" throughout the world, and because we read of the many casualties in armed conflict, and because we accept as a matter of fact the death toll on our highways—because of all that, have we hardened our hearts to the people who are crying out for our care? It is the Christian's duty never to be so much in a hurry that he isolates himself from aiding those who need his concern and love.

Love for Others

"I Knew You'd Come"

The story is told about two young men, in the last great war, who had been friends for their entire lifetimes. Being neighbors, they had played together, gone to school together, engaged in the same athletic programs, and finally had enlisted in the army together. Fate determined they would eventually be in the same area of battle together. After a particularly bitter battle one day it was found that one of the boys was missing somewhere out in what is known as "No Man's Land." The other boy, safe and unhurt, went to the commanding officer and requested permission to go out and look for his friend. He was told it was of no use for no one was alive out there after the withering fire of so many hours. After great insistence, he was finally given permission to go. Some time later he came back with the limp body of his friend over his shoulder. The commander said, "Didn't I tell you it was no use to go?" to which the boy replied with radiance in his eyes, "But it was. I got there in time to hear him whisper, 'I knew you'd come.'"

The above story is an example of the meaning of real friendship. Aristotle, the ancient Greek philosopher, once said, "A true friend is one soul in two bodies." The Lord, acknowledged Savior of the world, once said, "I have called you friends . . ." (John 15:15). No matter how much we may sentimentalize in human terms and relationships the matter of friendship, we can rest assured the heavenly friendship of God far surpasses all that any human is capable of attaining.

When trouble knocks at the door of our lives; when disappointments virtually overcome us and our plans and dreams; when tragedy strikes at the very heart of our existence; when life is just a frustrated maze of bewildering events—when all these things come upon us, we can rest assured that He is at our side offering solace, sympathy, and support. We need not worry whether "death's cold sullen stream" will submerge us.

The divine friendship the Lord has for us is to be reflected in our attitudes and actions toward our fellowman. A world filled with unrest and distrust needs friendship that is patiently and lovingly attempting to understand the wants and needs of others. It is looking at the faults and foibles of humanity and desiring to bring into lives the love of God. It is, as a little boy once said, knowing all about someone else and still liking him. It is the willingness to face danger, hurt, and harm in order that someone else will know there is loving care and concern in the hearts of others. It is the certainty that no matter what the situation, one can look up and say, "I knew you'd come."

Needed: More and Bigger Boats

The many tragedies at sea, caused by recent wars, and the heroic effort put forth to save the lives in each instance, calls to mind the disaster of "Princess Alice," which collided with another boat in a dense fog on the river Thames a little more than half a century ago. The boat was crowded with excursionists and the loss of human lives was great, about six hundred perishing in the dark waters. Dr. Herbert Lockyer tells of an interesting little sidelight of the tragedy which is worth repeating. It concerns two ferrymen.

It appears that these two ferrymen were mooring their boats for the night close at hand, when the crash happened. One heard the crash and the cries, and said, "I am tired and I am going home; no one will see me in the fog." At the coroner's inquest, both had to appear. The first was asked: "Did you hear the cries?" "Yes sir," replied the man. "What did you do?" "Nothing, sir." "Are you an Englishman?" asked the coroner, "and if so, aren't you ashamed?" "Sir," said the ferryman, "the shame will never leave me till I die." Turning to the other man, the question was put, "And you, sir, what did you do?" The second man replied in a simple and direct manner, "I jumped into my boat and pulled toward the wreck with all my might; I crammed my boat with women and children, and when it was too dangerous to take even one other, I rowed away with the cry, 'O God, for more and bigger boats.' "

In an age that seems to be completely frustrated and filled with fear; at a time when the masses are crying out for relief from uprisings and rest from war's bitter hatred, the gospel of love, as revealed in Jesus Christ, needs to be proclaimed over and over again. Many years ago, as the Man of Nazareth walked upon this earth and beheld the suffering of humanity, He cried out, "The harvest is plentiful, but the laborers are few; pray therefore the Lord of the harvest to send out laborers into his harvest." In other words, we too can repeat the ferryman's helpless cry, "O God, for more and bigger boats."

Is it possible that those who know the divine man, Jesus Christ, and who subscribe to Him and His principles of life, are so completely caught up with material activity and have become too "tired," and, therefore, have lost interest in the spiritual and moral welfare of their less fortunate brethren? We still need "more and bigger boats."

The Poet Was Inspired

A stranger was walking along a dusty road in New England. He was tired, hot, and worn. As he walked along that lonesome road he spied a small grove of trees. Taking time, he stopped to rest under the shade of one of them. As he was sitting there, he saw nearby a sign which read, "Here is a spring. If thirsty, drink!" After refreshing himself with the cool water, he walked further and saw a bench on which were painted the words: "If weary, rest on this bench!" Still further on he saw a basket of delicious apples and a sign which read, "If hungry, help yourself!"

"I must find out who does these nice things for strangers and passers-by," the stranger thought. Soon he came to an old hut. There sat an aged man whose face beamed kindness. "The blessings of the day to you," said the old man. "I have enjoyed the blessings placed by you along the dusty road. Why are you so kind and generous?" asked the traveler. The old man replied, "There are shade trees, benches, water, and fruit aplenty. So why not share them with strangers and weary travelers? God gives me great joy as I share what I have with others!"

The weary traveler on that dusty road was Sam Walter Foss. The old man's unselfishness and kindness to strangers inspired him to write the famous poem, "The House by the Side of the Road." The last verse of that poem reads,

> Let me live in my house by the side of the road
> Where the race of men go by—
> They are good, they are bad, they are weak, they are strong,
> Wise, foolish—so am I.
> Then why should I sit in the scorner's seat
> Or hurl the cynic's ban?—
> Let me live in my house by the side of the road
> And be a friend to man.

The admonition to those desiring to follow the example of Jesus Christ is clearly expounded in this statement, "So then, as we have opportunity, let us do good to all men" (Gal. 6:10). How much "poetry" could be written if there was more of this type of Christian concern!

The Ultimate in Love

It happened in one of the slum areas in a large city. A crippled girl underwent an operation that might enable her to walk again. After the operation, a long and tedious one, it was found that to keep her alive and make the surgery successful, the patient was in need of a blood transfusion. She had a rare type of blood and it seemed there was none available, until her fourteen-year-old brother volunteered his. Laboratory analysis certified that his blood matched. He was taken to the hospital and brought to the bedside of the crippled girl. The young, tough, disadvantaged fourteen-year-old school dropout and "troublemaker," looked on silently and tight-lipped as the vein in his arm was opened so that his blood might flow into the body of his unconscious sister. When the transfusion was completed the doctor put his hand on the boy's shoulder and complimented him on his brave conduct. The boy did not understand the doctor's action nor had he understood the nature of what a blood transfusion was. After a moment of silence he looked up and said, "Doc, how long will it be before I croak?" As far as he was concerned he had been dying, slowly and willingly. He expected his sister's continued living to mean his own death.

There, indeed, is the highest form of human love—sacrificing one's own life in behalf of another. "Greater love hath no man than this, that a man lay down his life for his friends" (John 15:13). In his human form the Savior, Jesus Christ, came that those who believe in Him might have life, and, as He said, "have it abundantly." Understanding our need, and fully aware of the cost of dying for a sinful world, the God-man entered into history and gave a complete "transfusion" to dying sinners. Remember, it was "complete." Just as a "blue baby" has all the blood removed from his system and has that blood replaced with new and healthy blood, so has the divine and loving heart of God made it possible to have "healthy blood"—reconciliation with Him—flow into the hearts and lives of those who are willing to receive the "transfusion." Every "operation" that is performed by the Great Physician can and will be totally successful. The results are (1) a new life in Christ; (2) a new attitude toward the living God that shows itself in a loyal following of Him; and (3) a new desire to glorify God through service to one's fellowman. The total giving to God of Himself for us is the ultimate in love.

Love for Others

"What a Change!"

When Jacob de Shazer went as one of Jimmy Doolittle's raiders on Japan on April 18, 1942, he was an atheist, believing in no God. During the air attack his plane was hit by enemy anti-aircraft bullets and he was forced to bail out. He was captured and imprisoned by the Japanese and thought certainly his life was approaching the end. He saw two of his companions shot by a firing squad and saw another die of slow starvation. During the long months of imprisonment he pondered the question of why the Japanese hated him and why he hated them. He began to recall some of the things he had heard about Christianity.

Boldly, he asked his jailers if they could get him a Bible. At first they laughed boisterously, as at a good joke, grew ugly, and warned him to stop making a nuisance of himself. But he kept asking. A year-and-a-half later—May 1944—a guard finally brought him a Bible, flung it at him, and said, "Three weeks you have. Three weeks, and then I take away." True to his word, in three weeks the guard took the Bible away and de Shazer never saw it again.

However, in those three weeks of intensive searching, meditating, and delving into the meaning of life and humanity's ultimate destiny, a change came about. Later he was released from Japanese captivity and returned home. In 1948, de Shazer, his wife, and infant son were on their way back to Japan *as missionaries,* all because he asked for a Bible and a Japanese guard gave him one for three weeks. He had searched the Scriptures and found life.

Many years ago, as the Son of God walked upon the face of the earth, He said to those within range of His voice, "You search the scriptures, because you think that in them you have eternal life; and it is they that bear witness to me; yet you refuse to come to me that you may have life" (John 5:39-40). And that truth still prevails. As man continues to search for ways and means to make a "better life" as well as give meaning to all that living is—and fails to find answers—the Word of God, the Bible, the revelation of God's will for His creation, still invites and beckons.

Where His Word has been heeded, where His Word has been accepted, where His Word has been lived, there transformations have taken place. The hardened criminal has been softened, the wayward child led home, the broken family reconciled, and the hopeless raised—all through the wonderful Word, Jesus Christ Incarnate, found in that sacred record preserved in the Bible. Can we do anything else except say, "What a change!" through the ever-living Word?

Materialism

The Danger of Wealth

A number of years ago, during the great "Gold Rush" in the United States, many people left the confines of safe and quiet dwellings to get rich quick by searching for gold, in what is now known as the State of California. In spite of many dangers involved, people piled their possessions in covered wagons, broke trails over the plains, fought hostile Indians, endured thirst in the desert, saw loved ones die, and continued to hope for a sudden "strike." Only a few were successful.

On one occasion, the story goes, a man found a lot of gold and decided to come back east to spend it and live in luxury and style. He wanted to be envied by those who were not brave enough to endure all the hardship. As he and others were crossing the Mississippi River in a "side-wheeler" it struck a rock and began to sink. The accident occurred close enough to shore to allow many who could swim to reach land and save themselves. However, many did drown, among them the man who had struck it rich. The survivors wondered why this had happened because he was supposed to have been an excellent swimmer. When the body was recovered from the water it was discovered that around his waist he had a belt of many pockets, all crammed with gold nuggets. The weight of the gold had dragged him down even though he was normally able to swim long distances. He could have removed the belt but he did not want to give up the wealth. He allowed it to carry him down to a watery grave.

There are countless numbers who behave just as that poor rich man did. Becoming so attached to their wealth, their material possessions, their "social security," and so much interested in the events of this world, they lose the most precious possession given to man—his everlasting soul. Many people become so engrossed in finding the "pot of gold" that health is lost, any ideal of value is shunted aside, and interest in God and the spiritual is forgotten. A futile and frustrated life results.

It was a terrible tragedy when the gold miner lost his life because he was unwilling to give up his gold. It is a greater tragedy when the "gold" of this world supplants all that is divine and eternal. The Lord once said, "For what shall it profit a man, if he shall gain the whole world, and lose his own soul?" (Mark 8:36 KJV). In the midst of an "affluent society," are we standing in danger of the wealth that surrounds us?

Materialism

Do You Fall for Bargains?

Perhaps it is not a very common practice, but there are some occasions when a storekeeper will take a nonselling article priced at 89c and mark it up to 98c, place a "Very Special Bargain" sign on it, and proceed to sell almost the entire lot. People are interested in "Bargains" whenever they go shopping. At a railroad depot, on the counter near the ticket office, was a large sign above some advertising folders. In large letters it said, "$5,000.00 for 25 cents!" Surely this was the kind of unheard-of "bargain" that comes but once in a lifetime! It bore looking into. When properly and carefully read the sign should have told the truth in the following manner: "$5,000.00 for 25c AND YOUR LIFE!" Or else, "$5,000.00 for 25c AND TWO EYES." Or again, "$5,000.00 for 25c AND BOTH HANDS!" The money part of the offer was much less attractive by the time the details were known. The fine print had to be read before one realized this was an insurance offer and that the only way to collect on the small sum of 25 cents investment was to lose one's life or become permanently disabled.

The chief antagonist to the Lord Jesus Christ and His way of life also offers "bargains" to the unsuspecting person in this world. Satan says: "The whole world can be yours if you will just worship me." What should be added to this false "bargain" are the words, "—and lose your soul eternally!" This is the danger the Lord had reference to when He said, "For what shall it profit a man if he shall gain the whole world and lose his own soul?'' (Mark 8:36 KJV).

In spite of the warnings against materialism and the temporary values found in this world there are great numbers who continue to shop at life's "Bargain Counters." Man yearns for that which glitters like gold . . . but evaporates like dew. True, lasting values, pure in their origination (in Jesus Christ) are by-passed for the tantalizing bittersweet fruit of a sinful desirous nature. It appears to be such a little bit to invest for "success" in the eyes of society. Forget God and His leadership. Forget loyalty to that One who brought life and immortality to light. Make all actions expedient to the situation. Latch onto those things that bring immediate joy to the physical senses. Be permissive. Be sensual. Take what you want. Separation from Christian fellowship is a small price to pay. Of course, you will have to forfeit your soul. It is possible to be fooled. Do *you* believe in bargains?

Materialism
It's Where You Look That Counts

"I thought it was a pretty fair telescope for one that wasn't very big," said Uncle Silas. "I rigged it up in the attic by the high north window, and had it fixed so it would swing easily. I took a great deal of satisfaction in looking through it—the sky seemed so wide and full of wonders; so when Hester was here I thought I'd give her the pleasure, too. She stayed a long time upstairs, and seemed to be enjoying it. When she came down I asked her if she had discovered anything new. Looking very pleased with herself and acting as though she has penetrated the secrets of the universe, she replied, 'Yes. Why, it made everybody's house so near that I seemed to be right beside them, and I found out what John Pritchard's folks are doing in their out-kitchen. I have wondered what they had a light there for night after night, and I just turned the glass on their windows and found out. They are cutting apples to dry—folks as rich as them cutting apples!' And actually that was all the woman had seen! With the entire heavens before her to study, she had spent her time looking into the affairs of her neighbors!''

Are we living in a "too-confined" world? As we evaluate our activities, is it possible that we have become so interested in looking into the "out-kitchens" of life that we forget the joy and privilege of seeing the Lord in all His glorious love and concern? The psalmist once wrote, "Thou hast said, 'Seek ye my face.' My heart says to thee, 'Thy face, Lord, do I seek'" (27:8). But we must ask ourselves the question, "Do I really seek the face of the Lord, or am I too interested in the material things that are at hand?" It is a question that is sometimes soul-disquieting. There are too many instances in life that show the honest lack of perceiving things as they are and placing them in correct priorities. Only when we realize the need of "seeing" the Lord will we begin to understand the vast panoramic view of God's mercy and love for us. Let us not be as the young man who once found a five-dollar bill on the street and from that time on never lifted his head while walking. In the course of years he accumulated 29,516 buttons, 54,172 pins, 12 cents, a bent back, and a miserable disposition. He lost the glory of the sunlight, the sheen of the stars, the smiles of his friends, the blossoms in the spring, the blue skies, and the entire joy of living. It's where you look that counts!

Materialism

What Do You Hear?

A scientist and a minister were walking in the midst of a throng of people on a crowded street. The scientist specialized in entomology—the study of insect life. Suddenly he stopped. "What do you hear?" he asked of the minister. "I hear the chatter of passing people, and the clangor and clatter of traffic," said the minister. "I hear a cricket above all the sounds you have mentioned," said the scientist. Going over to a nearby towering office building, he moved a small stone which lay against the foundation walls. Under it was a cricket, making its shrill music. "How could you hear it?" asked the preacher. "Very easily," said the scientist, "but let me show you something else." He led the preacher back into the center of the rushing crowds. "Now see what happens," he said, as he dropped a quarter on the cement. The quarter tinkled almost inaudibly in the noise of the passing traffic. But instantly some people stopped and listened! Said the scientist, "You hear what you want to hear and what you are trained to hear. You see what you want to see and what you are trained to see!"

In a world filled with much sound and fury; living in an age when the sound barrier is broken; listening to the horrendous noise of bursting bombs; confronted by the loud and raucous beat of "rock"—does the voice of the Lord become muted to our spiritual ears? Seeing death and destruction; observing class and mass struggle; noting inequality and inequities; having visualized, at our very doorsteps, crime and violence—is the Prince of Peace invisible to us? The Lord once asked His disciples the following: "Having eyes do you not see, and having ears do you not hear? And do you not remember?" (Mark 8:18). The desire of a loving God is eternally the same—to have His creatures observe this primary desire. But man has attuned himself to the temporary, the fading, the valueless.

When we consider, what is it we really want to see? What are the sounds that gain our attention? Do we want God's peace? Do we wish for true contentment? To have these desirable things we must both "hear" and "see" the Lord as He speaks through His holy Word.

Materialism

What Would You Rather Have?

It was in the thirties. Business curves were still heading downward and there was rumor of a salary cut at the New York insurance office where twenty-two-year-old Beverly Shea was employed as a clerk. Possessor of a deep melodious voice, the young man was offered a radio contract and immediately saw opportunities for fame and possible riches in his regular appearance on a secular program.

Shea had been pondering the matter for several days when he sat down to the piano early one Sunday morning to rehearse a hymn he was to sing in church that morning. As he played and sang his eyes fell on a piece of paper, on which was written:

> I'd rather have Jesus than silver or gold,
> I'd rather be His than have riches untold!

The poem, by Mrs. Rhea Miller, had been placed where Beverly would see it by his mother, a minister's wife, who knew of the offer her son was pondering. Above all, she wanted her son, a Christian, to become wholly consecrated to His service.

As his eyes raced over the words, the sentences "I'd rather have

Jesus than men's applause" and "I'd rather have Jesus than worldwide fame" struck his very heart. His fingers unconsciously left the tune he was rehearsing and began to find this melody which is today known to millions.

Several days afterward, the director who spoke to Shea in behalf of the radio network was amazed to receive a firm "no" in response to the offer. "No" was a strange word to the director's ear as thousands of singers would have leaped at such an opportunity as was proposed to the young bass-baritone. From that time forward, the words of the poem, "I'd Rather Have Jesus" set to music became his testimony. Today Shea is realizing his ambition to sing the gospel on radio and TV. He is sponsored on a hymn program, heard on many youth programs, and takes part in the Billy Graham Crusades.

"I'd rather have Jesus." Is this the sentiment of today's Christian? How often the temptation is set before the child of God to seek fame and fortune at any expense, even that of neglecting or rejecting the Lord! Paul speaks in words of commendation as, writing to the Corinthians, he mentions how the church of Macedonia "first . . . gave themselves to the Lord. . ." (II Cor. 8:5). When God is placed first, all other things fall into proper position. Then the matter of "priorities" is established. Would *you* rather have Jesus?

Memorial Day

Memorial Day! What thoughts come to your mind? What does the day mean to us and what do we remember? Just another "holiday"? Just a chance to take a day off from work and take the family for a ride, a picnic, with an all-day outing? Or is it an opportunity to spend the day on the golf course? What will we remember? Will we spend a few moments in silent thought and thanks for those who gave themselves that we might continue in the ways of democracy (which, by the way, means a system of government that considers the individual, regardless of color, race, or creed, important in the total scheme of things)? Or will we continue to thank God for our own position in life and forget there is no such thing as a "privileged class'?

The story is told about an incident which occurred when the first

Memorial Day was celebrated. A group of Washington D.C. women had asked the War Department for permission to put flowers on the soldiers' graves in Arlington Cemetery. After much persuasion, permission was granted, and on May 30th, the day designated, this was to be done. But a stern order was attached to the permission: No flowers were to be placed on the three hundred graves of the Confederate soldiers who were buried in a segregated section of the cemetery. The ladies who had made the request obediently decorated all the other graves, omitting the Confederate graves. Then General James A. Garfield made the speech at Arlington. When the crowd had left, a high wind rose. The wind blew almost all the flowers from the Union soldiers' graves into the Confederate area. After that day the separation was never again repeated.

The years have rolled by. Now, when the memory of the past is brought into focus, there is no distinction made between those who fought on one side or the other in support of the cause of freedom. Yet how often people forget that, in the sight of God and our country, all men are important and precious. Those who believe that this earth did not just come into being in an accidental way remember the words of Scripture when it states, "So God created man in his own image, in the image of God he created him; male and female he created them" (Gen. 1:27). The believer in God recognizes all humanity as God's creation—as the reflection of God's image. On Memorial Day must we not remember to honor the highest of all creation—man—with respect, dignity, consideration, and concern?

Mercy

The Penalty Was Paid

Two men who had been friends in their youth met later in the police court of one of our great metropolitan cities—one was sitting as judge of the court, the other stood before him as the prisoner, being tried for a serious traffic violation. The evidence was presented, heard, and deliberated upon, and the prisoner was found guilty. The ties of friendship were still strong between the two men. The sentiment of friendship would enter into the judge's verdict, it was believed by the prisoner. Looking down from the bench at his friend, the judge said, "I cannot fail to pass sentence upon you, my friend. That would not be justice. Justice must be done, and I must uphold the law." So he sentenced his friend, imposing a fifty-dollar fine, or thirty days in jail. The condemned man had nothing with which to pay, so prison was before him. Then the judge, having fulfilled his duty, stepped down beside the prisoner, paid his fine, put his arm around him, and said, "Now, John, you are coming home with me to dinner!"

Every person shall, at some point in his history, stand before the eternal Judge, the holy and perfect God. Evidence will be presented that will show him guilty of violating the divine Law, for we read in Scripture, "Surely there is not a righteous man on earth who does good and never sins" (Eccles. 7:20) and also, ". . . all have sinned and fall short of the glory of God" (Rom. 3:23). The righteous and perfect God will have no choice but to pronounce the verdict of "Guilty." However, there is another side of the heavenly courtroom scene. Just as the judge stepped down from the bench and paid the fine of the traffic violater who had nothing to meet the cost, so does the heavenly Judge figuratively step down and "pay" the fine of each guilty person who stands before Him but who has placed his faith in the active and atoning work of Jesus Christ in his behalf. Paul says, "They are justified by his grace as a gift, through the redemption which is in Christ Jesus, whom God put forward as an expiation by his blood, to be received by faith. This was to show God's righteousness, because in his divine forbearance he had passed over former sins; it was to prove at the present time that he himself is righteous and that he justifies him who has faith in Jesus" (Rom. 3:24-26). For those who believe in Jesus Christ as Lord and Savior, they find that when their day in court arrives "the penalty has been paid!" Thank God that in divine love He has brought to His creatures eternal life in and through His Son.

Mother's Day

Reflections on Mother's Day

As someone once said, "Isn't it strange that one day of the year is set aside to honor mothers, while on the other hand, we have a Pickle *Week?*" Nevertheless, mothers certainly are honored much more than one day a year. Or are they? If they are not thought of in loving ways by their children, it would seem one of two reasons must be given. Either they are unworthy of love or there are unthinking and unloving children. Looking forward to the celebration of Mother's Day, the following thoughts come to mind:

A teacher once said to a little boy, "James, suppose your mother made a peach pie, and there were ten of you at the table—your mother and father and eight children—how much of the pie would you get?"

"A ninth, ma'am," James answered.

"No, no, James, pay attention," said the teacher. "There are ten of you—ten, remember? Don't you know your fractions?"

"Yes, ma'am," said James. "I know my fractions, but I know my mother, too. She'd say she didn't want no pie!"

An aged, white-haired mother sat with a smile on her face in the White House, waiting for her famous son, Dwight, to arrive. Someone said to her, "You must be very proud of your great and illustrious son." Upon which she asked, "Which son?" Each one was equally great to that noble mother—Dwight D. Eisenhower's mother.

Dr. G. Campbell Morgan had four sons. They all became ministers. At a family reunion, a friend asked one of the sons, "Which Morgan is the greatest preacher?" While the son looked at the father, he replied, "Mother!"

A mother was asked: "Which of your thirteen children do you love the most?" She replied, "The one who is sick, until he gets well, and the one who is away, until he gets home."

Holy Scripture has words of praise for the godly mother. Among the many expressions that befit Mother's Day is that which says, "Her children rise up and call her blessed; her husband also, and he praises her" (Prov. 31:28). Let us honor the godly mothers on their day!

Mother's Day

"A Tribute to Mothers"

A very beautiful story is related of a boat out at sea carrying in it a father and his little daughter. As they were steering for the shore they were overtaken by a violent storm which threatened to destroy them. The coast was dangerous. The mother, at the home by the seashore, lighted a lamp and started up the worn stairway to the attic window.

"It won't do any good, mother," the son called after her. But the mother went up, put the light in the window, knelt beside it and prayed. Out in the storm the daughter saw a glimmer of gold on the water's edge. "Steer for that," the father said. Slowly but steadily they came toward the light, and at last were anchored in the little sheltered harbor by the cottage. "Thank God," cried the mother, as she heard their glad voices and came down the stairway with a lamp in her hand. "How did you get here?" she asked. "We steered by mother's light," answered the daughter, "although we did not know what it was out there.

"Aha!" thought the boy, who was not known for being a very decent type of person, "aha, it is time I was steering by mother's light." And before he went to sleep that night he surrendered himself to God and asked Him to guide him over life's rough seas. Months went by, and finally the boy was discovered to have an incurable disease. The doctor carefully examined him and just shook his head hopelessly. It was another stormy night when the doctor came for the last time. "He can't live long," was his verdict. The dying young man looked up into the troubled faces and said, "Do not be afraid for me. I shall make the harbor, for I have been steering by mother's light.

The Word of God advises each person, "And do not despise your mother. . ." (Prov. 23:22b). In an age where respect is so seemingly lacking, it is evident that honor to one's mother is also passé and antiquated. Yet there are countless numbers of men, world famous, who have paid the highest tribute possible to their mothers. Abraham Lincoln once said, "All that I am, or hope to be, I owe to my angel mother." An old saying, theologically unsound, yet expressing a deep respect for mothers and motherhood, says, "God could not be everywhere, so he made mothers."

As we approach Mother's Day let those homes that have the shining example of Christian living in mother's daily life and activity truly thank God for this rich blessing that money cannot buy. For others who are willing to sacrifice all for the family let us thank the God who sacrificed all in behalf of humanity in the person of Jesus Christ.

Making Tracks

One day two little boys were enjoying the first heavy snowfall of the season. As is the practice with so many children when they get carried away with the season, they threw snowballs, made several snowmen, rolled a big snowball until it was so large they could no longer push it, and rode their sleds down any hill that could be found. After a while, one of the boys said, "Let's see who can make the straightest tracks across that field." So, over the road they went and started to plow through the field that was snow covered and trackless. When they got to the other side of the field and looked back, it could be seen that one boy made an almost straight path while the other one's tracks were crooked and zig-zagged. Discussing the difference in the two sets of tracks, the one asked the other, "Why were yours so straight while mine were crooked?" The second boy answered, "It's very simple. I picked out a certain post on the other side of the field and kept my eyes on it, always walking straight toward it." A plain and simple statement of fact. One had looked down or around resulting in an all-directional wandering while the other boy chose a goal and kept his eyes on it.

Paul, writing to the Philippians (3:14 KJV) said: "I press toward the mark for the high calling of God in Christ Jesus." His one goal and aim in life was to reach the ultimate source of a meaningful life. This, he knew, could only be accomplished by keeping his eye on the "prize"—companionship and comradeship with a living and loving Christ. As far as the great New Testament writer was concerned, he counted anything and everything else but loss!

In today's world we are invited and urged to set many goals for ourselves. We are told security lies in amassed wealth, social position, political connections, and/or economic prestige. Having tried one or all of these methods we look back and discover the days of our lives have had an "all-directional wandering." Certainty and security elude us. Instead of "always walking straight" toward the "prize"—a life guided by the Lord—we have spent much of our time aimlessly and fruitlessly engaged in unrewarding activity.

As the year lies ahead should we not, must we not, get our "bearings" and live lives that are useful and that have meaning? How else can it be done except to "press toward the mark for the prize of the high calling of God in Christ Jesus?'' Let it be known that we are making tracks that are straight.

Obedience

Forward March!

A young GI, just returned from fulfilling his military obligation, attended a special worship service at his home church. In his dress uniform, with various medals on it, he was very impressive looking. The pastor of the congregation noticed him among the members and invited him to come to the front of the church and speak a few words to those present. As he came forward the congregation anticipated some statements concerning the war and the experiences he had personally met. However, the GI began speaking in the following manner:

'' 'Like a mighty army moves the church of God!' The trouble is that over ten million men know exactly how an army moves. Suppose the army accepted the lame excuses that many a church member thinks good enough for not attending the church parade. Imagine this happening: Reveille at 7 A.M.—squads on parade ground. The sergeant barks out, 'Count fours.' 'One, two, three'—four is missing. 'Where's Private Smith?' Someone answers, 'Mr. Smith was too sleepy to get up. He said to tell you he would be with you in spirit.' 'Where's Brown?' the sergeant says. 'He's playing golf. You know how important recreation is.' 'Sure, sure,' says the sergeant cheerfully. 'Hope he has a good game. Where's Robinson?' 'Oh, he is so sorry, but he is entertaining guests today. Besides, he was at drill last week.' 'Will you please tell him he is welcome any time he finds it convenient to drop in for drill,' replies the sergeant. Why, if any GI pulled that stuff he would get twenty days in the brig. Yet you hear stuff like that every week in the church. 'Like a mighty army!' If the church moved like a mighty army, a lot of folks would be court-martialed within an hour.'' Looking over the audience, the young soldier's concluding remarks were, ''I would suggest the refrain to 'Onward Christian Soldiers' should be sung with the following words: 'Onward Christian soldiers, Going on to war, With the cross of Jesus still behind the door.''' Without another word he took his place in the pew where he had been sitting. The congregation remained motionless and at the close of the service left the church with very few words spoken between individuals. Somehow there seemed to be an aura of guilt surrounding them.

Jesus once told His disciples, "If any man would come after me, let him deny himself and take up his cross, and follow me" (Matt. 16:24). The Christian faith is dynamic. It is a force that moves forward, overcoming all obstacles, with the spirit and power of its Master. Today, every day, the world needs to see the church of Jesus Christ performing its task—the proclamation of reconciliation of man and God through the only known Savior. The word is out—Forward March!

Obedience

I Broke Its Leg!

One day a lady, vacationing in Switzerland, started out for a stroll that ended part way up the mountainside. She came to a shepherd's fold, walked to the door and looked in. There she saw the shepherd, and around him lay his flock. Near at hand, on a pile of straw, lay a single sheep. It seemed to be in great suffering. Looking more closely, the lady saw that its leg was broken. With sympathy in her voice she asked the shepherd, "How did it happen?" To her amazement, the shepherd answered, "Madam, I broke that sheep's leg." The look on her face clearly displayed her thoughts about such cruel and inhumane treatment. Seeing that look, the shepherd went on, "Lady, of all the sheep in my flock, this one was the most wayward. It never would obey my voice; would never follow in the pathway in which I was leading the flock. It wandered to the verge of many a perilous cliff and dizzy abyss; and was not only disobedient itself, but was ever leading other sheep of my flock astray. I had had experiences before with sheep of this kind. So I broke its leg. The first day I went to it with food, it tried to bite me. I let it lie alone for a couple of days. Then, I went back to it. And now, it not only took the food, but licked my hand, and showed every sign of submission and even affection. And now let me tell you something. When the sheep is well, as it soon will be, it will be the model sheep of my flock. No sheep will hear my voice as quickly. None will follow as closely at my side."

Many times people are quick to fault the wisdom and actions of a totally good and concerned God. Many are the times when those within the "sheep-fold" of the Master and Savior are angry at the Lord for suffering and sorrow that may be inflicted upon them. Many are the times mortal man questions immortal God as to His purposes. Scripture assures us, in the Lord's own words, "I am the Good Shepherd; I know my own and my own know me" (John 10:14). Anything and everything that is done, and that happens, God uses for His own glory and man's ultimate good. A sage has said, "Often it is necessary for a man to be knocked flat on his back before he looks up."

In a day and age when "affluence" is a household word and "good times" and the feeling of complete independence is evidenced, waywardness from God becomes the accepted way of life. Do you think that perhaps when we are visited with difficulties the Lord is attempting to bring us to realize our need for Him? Just maybe, for our eternal welfare God, in love, says, "I broke its leg."

Obedience

There Is Power in Obedience

Many an illustrious event took place in the life of the Duke of Wellington, that great and famous man in the Empire of Great Britain. On one occasion, the farmers of the land were complaining of the huntsmen galloping over their fields, and they resolved to keep them out. They locked the gates, then posted men and boys at the gates. Up came a member of the Duke of Wellington's hunting party. There stood the little farmer boy. The gentleman said, "Open the gate!" "I must not," replied the boy. By that time, up came the Duke himself. The gentleman said, "Your grace, that boy refuses to open the gate." The Duke looked down and said, "My boy, open it!" "I must not," again replied the boy. "Do you know who I am?" asked the Duke. The little fellow said nervously, "I believe you are Mr. Duke of Wellington." "Won't you open the gate for me?" "My master told me to open it to nobody." The Duke was so pleased with the boy's implicit obedience that he handed him a sovereign, which is equivalent to a five-dollar bill. As the Duke rode away, the little fellow was overjoyed with the present, and sat on the top of the gate waving his cap at the departing party. He had done what Napoleon and his army could not do; he had kept the Duke of Wellington out of the fields.

There was a time in the early history of the Christian church when the apostles of the Lord were forbidden to preach the new religion of Jesus of Nazareth. They were arrested, placed in prison, brought before the authorities, threatened, beaten, and warned to refrain from further referral to the One who had been crucified but who had risen on the third day. However, the reply of Peter, the spokesman for the group, was this, "We must obey God rather than men" (Acts 5:29). And they went forth and continued the proclamation of the love of God, found and revealed in Jesus Christ. They suffered indignities and physical torture, and finally death was their reward. But they were obedient to the command to "go preach and teach."

The modern-day Christian also has the imperative given to him to live and proclaim by word and action the same love of the same and changeless Savior. Believing in the power of Almighty God surely those who claim Him will obey His will and desire. His way will resist the evil that surrounds us in the world!

Obedience

The Voice Was Heard

During the First World War several Turkish soldiers attempted to drive away a flock of sheep while their shepherd was sleeping nearby. This occurred on a hillside near Jerusalem on a warm and pleasant day. The shepherd was suddenly aroused and saw his sheep being driven off by the Turkish soldiers. The keeper of the flock was sympathetic to the British and their cause, and besides, he did not want to lose his sheep. Singlehanded, he could not hope to recapture his sheep by force. The enemy soldiers would not only keep his sheep but would most likely kill him, or at least, take him prisoner and force him to labor as a prisoner.

Suddenly the shepherd had an idea. Standing on his side of the ravine, a safe distance from the soldiers, he put his hand to his mouth and gave his own peculiar call to gather his sheep. As the voice echoed and reechoed through the ravine, the sheep heard it, listened for a moment, then hearing the call resound again they turned and rushed down one side of the ravine and up the other. It was quite impossible for the Turkish soldiers to stop them, and they could not rush down the ravine in headlong fashion. The shepherd escaped with his sheep to a place of safety before the soldiers had decided what to do. There was only one voice that held authority and familiarity for those sheep, and it was the one that belonged to the person who had led them over treacherous countryside safely and found food, water, and refuge in the wilderness. No other voice could command their attention and have them follow. The voice was clear and distinct. They had heard it before, and they knew that the owner of that voice would assure tender care.

Jesus, speaking to those who followed Him, said, ". . . the sheep hear his voice, and he calls his own sheep by name and leads them out. When he has brought out all his own, he goes before them, and the sheep follow him, for they know his voice" (John 10:3-4). In the middle of a confused world with its many "voices" the follower of the Master heeds only the one authoritative voice that has loving concern. But it is important that the "sheep" know that voice. One only "knows" if he has learned to listen. What voice do you follow? Do you recognize that one who lives and cares? And if you hear, do you follow?

Patriotism

America Can Remain Great

The life, time, and activity of George Washington, during the trying days of the Revolutionary War, at Valley Forge, is common knowledge to most children and adults who have studied any part of the history of the United States. General Washington was one man who found rest and relief in prayer, and it was not an uncommon sight for his soldiers to see him on bended knee seeking strength, guidance, and courage. With all the cares and anxieties of that time resting on him, he felt the presence of God most needful in his titanic struggle for the freedom of the newly established nation. One day a farmer approaching the camp heard an earnest voice. On coming nearer, he saw George Washington on his knees, his cheeks wet with tears, praying to God. The farmer returned home and said to his wife: "George Washington will succeed! George Washington will succeed! The Americans will secure their independence!"

"What makes you think so, Issac?" asked the wife. The farmer replied: "I heard him pray, Hannah, out in the woods today, and the Lord will surely hear his prayer. He will, Hannah; thou may rest assured He will." And history records the fact well. Washington, and the courageous men who fought bloody battles, succeeded to bring to the American continent a new nation "under God."

It would appear, in this present age and generation, that little concern is being given by many in high places in government, to moral strength and God-guidance. While many lands cry out in destitution and poverty, and while our own United States basks in great wealth and material affluence, leadership too often acts as though all of this is man's doing alone. And the rank and file of the population lives as though there is "no tomorrow" and no accounting necessary. The greatness of America was not founded, built, and enlarged with that type of philosophy. There is no such thing as "privileged class" or nation, in the sight of God; except as the apostle Peter once wrote, "God shows no partiality, but in every nation any one who fears him and does what is right is acceptable to him" (Acts 10:34-35).

To continue to have the joys and privileges we now enjoy must we not remember to hold fast to the fundamental principles of our land? To remain great in God's sight and respected by other nations and lands, must we not trust God and live according to His desires and rules which are honesty, concern, fairness, justice, mercy, compassion, and peace? Let us look to God for guidance and help and live lives that will keep America great!

Patriotism

The Meaning of "Freedom"

Charles A. Lindbergh, the "Lone Eagle," in his book, *Of Flight and Life*, states, "To me in youth, science was more important than either man or God. I worshiped science. I was awed by its knowledge. Its advances had surpassed man's wildest dreams. In its learning seemed to lie the key to all mysteries of life.

"It took many years for me to discover that science, with all its brilliance, lights only a middle chapter of creation. I saw the science I worshiped, and the aircraft I loved, destroying the civilization I expected them to serve, and which I thought as permanent as earth itself. Now I understand that spiritual truth is more essential to a nation than the mortar in its cities walls. For when the actions of a people are unguided by these truths, it is only a matter of time before the walls themselves collapse. The most urgent mission of our time is to understand these truths and to apply them to our way of modern life. We must draw strength from the almost forgotten virtues of simplicity, humility, contemplation, prayer. It requires dedication beyond science, beyond self, but the rewards are great and it is our only hope.''

The Lord God has said, ''If my people humble themselves, and pray, and seek my face, and turn from their wicked ways, then will I hear from heaven, and will forgive their sin and heal their land'' (II Chron. 7:14). He urges the nations to look to the living Lord, seek guidance, acknowledge need for humility and love, and practice concern and compassion on fellowmen. It takes a great nation to practice humility in God's sight, surrender to Him, and thereby find the real meaning to ''freedom.''

The inscription on the Plymouth Rock monument is a challenge to every generation of Americans: ''This spot marks the final resting place of the Pilgrims of the 'Mayflower.' In weariness and hunger and cold, fighting the wilderness and burying their dead in common graves that the Indians should not know how many had perished, they here laid the foundations of a state in which all men for countless ages should have liberty to worship God in their own way. All you who pass by and see this stone remember, and dedicate yourselves anew to the resolution that you will not rest until this lofty ideal shall have been realized through out the earth.''

Peace with God

How Does One Describe ''Peace''?

Two artists put upon canvas their concepts of peace. One artist painted a placid rural scene in the center of which was a country home. Adjacent to the home were fertile fields and an abundant harvest. The undulating roads stretched in different directions from the home toward the horizon. A lazy haze hovered over glen and dale. One could almost hear the rustle of the ripened wheat, swayed with the kiss of the gentle breeze. A friendly sun shone

89

upon the blissful picture of calm and contentment. Cows lay lazily under a shade tree, chewing their cuds.

The other artist gave a totally different concept of peace. A destroying tempest raged in his painting. Trees swayed to and fro on the storm-lashed mountainside and in the valley. The sky was ominous and gloomy, relieved only by the zigzag flashes of lightning. A roaring waterfall lunged furiously over the precipice, working disaster in the valley below! Why could the artist call this violent, turbulent scene a representation of peace? On a rock projecting from the cliff, sheltered by an overhanging boulder, a little bird sat calmly on its nest, seemingly unmindful of the howling storm or of the raging waters which plunged downward nearby. There the little bird sat in peace, with no fear, unperturbed and undisturbed!

There is no question that humanity lives in a world that is filled with skies that are "ominous and gloomy." "Lightning" flashes across the countryside of life in forms of violence, hatred, bitterness, discontent, and disappointment. There seems to be no escape from the strain, stress, and storms of life. Man cries out desperately for "Peace" and it is nowhere to be found —apparently. Yet we are told in God's Word, the Holy Bible, "Thou [God] will keep him in perfect peace, whose mind is stayed on thee: because he trusteth in thee" (Isa. 26:3 KJV). Is it just possible the reason for the instability of the world is due to the fact that there is so little searching with one's mind and heart for the God of creation and redemption? Could it be that man has become so enamored with himself he forgets to look to the only One who can offer and make peace a reality? It is a child of God who can be as the bird in the second artist's concept of peace. He knows there is no fury in the world that can separate him from divine love and compassion. "Peace" is standing in correct relationship to God!

Peace with God

The Sound of Silence

Just recently a simple observation was made, one so simple that it was frightening in its profundity. Some place between the reality of consciousness and the dream world of sleep is the area of fantasy. In this "Twilight Zone" of the mind I saw "strange" but familiar sights, and "heard" sounds ordinarily not recognized in the light of day. I found myself in a city totally strange and yet vaguely familiar, walking on a street I had never walked before, and seeing sights and hearing music and voices that were "different" yet somehow ordinary. In a broad panoramic view there were orchestras playing everything from Bach to "Bop." Dancers were sedately gliding across ballroom floors and also wildly gyrating like whirling dervishes. Peddlers were hawking their wares, people were fervishly buying, men were seemingly expectant, and women were apparently apprehensive. Children huddled furtively behind the shadows cast by fearsome towers. Everything was in a state of unrest. Feeling detached from the scene, I looked about for something that would give evidence of safety and security. Nothing seemed to be, or had to offer, any assurance. The blending of sounds was impossible—harmony of motion could not be accomplished. I saw and heard the terrible "Sound of Confusion."

Then it happened! Without a bit of forewarning the cacaphony of noises ceased. Stopped! Complete nothingness! A far greater "sound" reached my ears—it was the "Sound of Silence"! Not gradually—a bit at a time. All at once! No music from the orchestras was heard. No songs from the lips of the singers. No gliding or gyrating feet of dancers. No sounds from the peddlers. Nothing but the "Sound of Silence!" It was eerie. It was mind-defying and soul-disturbing. Try as hard as human effort allowed but nothing but the "Sound of Silence!" Fear and foreboding were evidenced on every single face, well, almost every face, for I saw a child emerge from the shadow with a face so radiantly calm and peaceful that everything else fell into the background. Apparently this child could walk confidently toward a dim but steady light shining in the distance. And then it dawned on me. The wonderful "Sound of Silence" was the invitation of the Lord God who had said, "Be still and know that I am God" (Ps. 46:10). He overcomes the "Sound of Confusion" with peace in the glorious and restful "Sound of Silence" in Christ our Lord.

"Lord, to whom shall we go? thou hast the words of eternal life. And we believe and are sure that thou art that Christ, the Son of the living God" (John 6:68-69).

There Is a Need for Peacemakers

There is a story told concerning two members of a church that had disagreed over a very trivial and unimportant matter. The disagreement continued over a period of time until it hardened into ill will and hatred. A mutual friend became distressed about the situation and finally said to himself, "I'm going to be a peacemaker and do what I can to heal the breach between my friends." He called on his friend Brown first and asked him, "What do you think of my friend Thompson?" Brown looked at him, and in anger answered: "Think of him? He is contemptible in my sight!" The peacemaker replied, "But you must admit he is very kind to his family." Somewhat hesitantly came the answer, "Yes, that's true. He is kind to his family." The next day the peacemaker called to see his friend Thompson and said, "Do you know what Brown said about you?" "No, but I can imagine the dirty, unkind things he would say about me!" "Well," said the peacemaker, "he said you are very kind to your family." "What! Did he say that?" exclaimed Thompson. "He surely did. Now, what do you think of Thompson?" Brown said, "I think he is a scamp and a rascal." The peacemaker continued, "But you will have to admit that he is an honest man." "Yes, he is honest, but what has that to do with it?" The very next day the peacemaker called on Thompson and said, "Do you know that Brown said that you are a very honest man?" "You don't mean it," said Thompson. "I do mean it. I heard him say it with my own ears." The next Sunday, Brown and Thompson sat together in church, rejoicing in each other's fellowship. The attempt of the peacemaker was successful!

From the wonderful Sermon on the Mount, Jesus is quoted as saying, "Blessed are the peacemakers, for they shall be called sons of God" (Matt. 5:9). There is much tension in the world today. Individuals as well as classes and groups of people, nations, and races are at each other's throats. We desperately stand in need of those who would bring harmony where there is discord and tranquillity where there is tumult. If only each person would take time in his own little sphere and bring together those who are separated by misunderstanding and bitterness. If only those of us who appreciate the love of God would make more of an effort to find good in those who are hurting because of hatred! Are you one of the sons of God—are you a peacemaker?

"Hold the Fort, I Am Coming"

In Sherman's march from Chattanooga to Atlanta and the sea, General Johnson was removed from his command by the Confederates, and his army given to the impetuous General Hood. Hood at once marched to the rear of Sherman, threatening his communications and base of supplies at Allatoona, which commanded the pass through the mountains. Sherman sent an order to one of his lieutenants, Corse, to proceed to Allatoona. He himself went as far back as Kenesaw Mountain, and from that eminence on the clear October day could see plainly the smoke of battle and hear the faint reverberation of the cannon.

His flag officer at length made out the letters which were being wigwagged from the garrison at Allatoona, "Corse is here." This was a great relief to Sherman, who then heliographed his famous message, "Hold the fort, I am coming." Among the soldiers in Sherman's army was a young officer, Major Whittle, who related the incident to P. P. Bliss, the famous evangelist. Taking this incident as his inspiration, Bliss wrote the once well-known gospel hymn, "Hold the Fort, for I Am Coming."

There is no doubt that the Christian in the world is filled with uncertainty, fear, and dismay. However, no matter how difficult the situation, there is one great assurance for him, and that is: "The Lord will return!" In the Gospel of John, the Lord, speaking words of comfort to His followers, said, "Let not your hearts be troubled, neither let them be afraid. You heard me say to you, 'I go away, and I will come to you' " (14:27-28). In the meantime the people of God are to be found occupying positions of loyalty to Him by continuing to witness to divine truth.

Where the cries of a helpless humanity are heard, the army of God must move forward to aid; where the moans of sorrow and anguish are raised toward heaven, the sympathetic follower of Christ must attempt to ease the burden; where hatred rears its heartless head, the professing Christian must show love, concern, and understanding of the problems caused by sin. All this is to be done because one honestly believes the word of his Lord and King, who said, "I will come to you." The enemy forces are not so great as to overcome. We rely on Him who is our King. He has said, "Hold the fort. I am coming!"

93

No Time to Stop

How Captain Cook and his party of faithful followers set out on their trip in search of the North Pole, is always an interesting story. Dr. Solander, a learned Swede, and also a man of exceedingly peppery temper, accompanied them in the capacity of naturalist. It was the depth of winter, and a cold south wind, accompanied by driving snow, surprised the explorers when some considerable distance from their encampment. Dr. Solander, therefore, called the party around him, and his face grew grave. "I have had some experience of this in my own country," he said, "but you have had none. Now, listen to this piece of advice, for upon it depends your lives. We must resolutely set our faces to get back to the encampment, and with never a stop, for the danger lies in falling asleep."

"I suppose we shall get horribly tired, doctor?" asked Lieutenant Hodder, the leader of the party, trying to smile at the unpleasant prospect. "Of course we shall," answered the quick-tempered doctor sharply, "but it will be a chance to see what we are made of. I warn you, Hodder, that the men, as their blood grows cold, will ask to be allowed to rest. Do not permit it for a moment—urge them—urge them with blows, with the bayonet, if necessary! Remember, the wish to stop is the first symptom of the blood refusing to circulate. To yield to it is death!"

The party moved on: the wind blew, and snow fell, and the frost cut them through and through, yet their stout hearts held on still. There was no wish expressed to stop, and if any felt a longing for rest, none voiced that longing, but suppressed it and kept it under by firm, dogged will power.

There is always the temptation in life to "give up" doing that which is right and proper, especially when it appears the action and endeavor is not appreciated, or refused. The Christian person finds himself facing the spiritual cold winds and heavy snows of people who laugh and make light of moral courage and determination. The blood runs cold and the inclination is to stop and rest, or worse, retire from the scene. Paul, shortly before his death, said, "I have fought the good fight, I have finished the race, I have kept the faith" (II Tim. 4:7). As long as there is a breath of life within the man of God, he will not become discouraged, nor will he willingly "give in" to the inroads of worldly godlessness. Christian principles and ethics are needed in this age. No matter what the odds, there's "No Time to Stop!"

Prayer

Just Coincidence?

Captain Johnson was serving as chaplain on an island in the South Pacific during World War II. He prepared to go on a bombing raid on enemy-occupied islands several hundred miles away. The mission was a complete success, but on the homeward course the plane began to lose altitude and the engines faded out. A safe landing was made on a strange island. It was learned later that the enemy was just one-half mile in each direction, yet the landing had gone undetected. The staff sergeant came to the chaplain and said, "Chaplain, you have been telling us for months of the need of praying and believing God answers prayer in time of trouble, and that He does it right away. We're out of gas, base several hundred miles away—almost surrounded by the enemy." Johnson began to pray and lay hold of the promises and believed that God would work a miracle. Night came and the chaplain continued his intense prayer. About 2 A.M. the sergeant awakened and felt compelled to walk to the water's edge. He discovered a metal float, which had drifted up on the beach—a barge on which were fifty barrels of high-octane gas. In a few hours the crew reached their home base safely. An investigation revealed that the skipper of a U.S. tanker, finding his ship in sub-infested waters, had his gasoline cargo removed so as to minimize the danger in case of a torpedo hit. Barrels were placed on barges and put adrift six hundred miles from where Johnson and the plane crew were forced down. God had nagivated one of these barges through wind and current and beached it fifty steps from the stranded men. Coincidence?

In the New Testament Letter of James, the inspired writer said, "The prayer of a righteous man has great power in its effects" (5:16b). In a world filled with blasé and sophisticated people, the thought may be that no longer does one place confidence in the calling upon God for deliverance. Unless one has the detailed plan laid before him, his hopes and his dreams are just that—hopes and dreams. There can be no telling of gain through the "superstitious incantations" of a simple, benighted mind that believes in the efficacy of prayer. But how true it is, as Ethel Romig Fuller writes,

If radio's slim fingers can pluck a melody
From night—and toss it over a continent or sea;
If the petalled white notes of a violin
Are blown across the mountains or the city's din;
If songs, like crimson roses, are culled from thin blue
    air—
Why should mortals wonder if God hears prayer?

Prayer

Power to Overcome

The Greek writer, Homer, tells us that when Ulysses came to the Aegean isle where the daughter of the sun, Circe, lived, he climbed a hill and saw in the center of the island a palace surrounded with trees. He sent one half of his crew, under the command of Eurylochus, as a vanguard, to see if he could find hospitality. When the men approached the palace, which was surrounded by wild animals that had once been men now changed into beasts by Circe's witchcraft, they heard the sounds of soft music from within. When they entered—all but their leader Eurylochus, who suspected danger—Circe served them with wine and other delicacies. When they had eaten and drunk heartily she touched them one by one with her wand, and they were immediately changed into swine.

When Eurylochus brought the story of this disaster to Ulysses, he went forth to rescue his men. As he was going, he was met on the way by Mercury, who warned him of the dangerous arts of Circe. But as Ulysses would not be put off from his wish to save his men, Mercury put in his hand a flower, the fragrance of which he was to inhale, which had the power to resist all sorceries. Armed with this flower, Ulysses entered the palace of Circe, who entertained him as she had his companions; and when he had eaten and drunk, she touched him with her wand, saying, "Hence, seek the sty and wallow with thy friends!" But protected from her spell by the flower which he carried, Ulysses drew his sword and compelled her to release his companions and restore them to their human form.

The man or woman who entertains high thoughts, is moral in his approach to the problems his fellowmen have, who is desirous of raising the standards of justice, truth, and righteousness, and who would stave off the sorcery of modern "Circes," can look to only one source of strength—the Almighty God, through the wonderful medium of prayer. The finest example of the effectiveness of prayer was given by the Son of God, Jesus Christ, when just before His betrayal He prayed in the Garden of Gethsemene. We read, "And he withdrew from them [the disciples] about a stone's throw, and knelt down and prayed. . . .And there appeared to him an angel from heaven, strengthening him" (Luke 22:41, 43). So encouraged He continued to the cross and overcame all human threats and obstacles. We have the same opportunity to have power to overcome our human weaknesses and the temptations of this world—not the flower of Mercury, but the powerful word of prayer, in His name!

Prayer

Should You Use a Chair?

The story is told of an old Scotsman whose minister came to see him as he lay very ill in bed. As the minister sat down on a chair near the bedside he noticed on the other side of the bed another chair placed at such an angle as to suggest that another visitor had just left it. "Well, Donald," said the clergyman, "I see I am not your first visitor." The Scotsman looked up in surprise; so the minister pointed to the chair. "Ah," said the sufferer. "I'll tell you about that chair. Years ago I found it impossible to pray. I often fell asleep on my knees, I was so tired. And if I kept awake, I could not control my thoughts from wandering. One day I was so worried I spoke to my minister about it. He told me not to worry about kneeling down. 'Just sit down,' he told me, 'and put a chair opposite you, and imagine Jesus is in it, and talk to Him as you would to a friend.' " The man added, "I have been doing that ever since. And so, now you know why the chair is standing like that."

A week later the daughter of the old Scot drove up to the minister's house and knocked at the door. She was shown into the study, and when the minister came in she could hardly restrain herself. "Father died in the night," she sobbed. "I had no idea death could be so near. I had just gone to lie down for an hour or two, for he seemed to be sleeping so comfortably. And when I went back he was dead. He had not moved since I saw him before, except that his hand was on the empty chair at the side of the bed. Do you understand?" said the daughter. "Yes," said the minister, "I understand."

For those who truly desire to be in communication with God, and who realize the importance of a life of prayer, know the psalmist was correct when he said, "But truly God has listened; he has given heed to the voice of my prayer" (Ps. 66:19). The posture in prayer is unimportant in the eye and mind of God. All that is needed is that personal realization that He who created and loves His creatures is desirous of having them approach Him in a vital and sincere manner. Maybe to make prayer more meaningful one should follow the example of the Scotsman who found he could honestly talk to God as he sat "facing" Him chair to chair. Could it be we might benefit by this practice? How wonderful to fall asleep comfortably and assured of His nearness. And how peaceful it could be to us to touch that chair where our heavenly Father "sits" listening as we pour our hearts out to Him in the privacy of our room. Should we have a chair pulled up for Him in our prayer sessions?

Procrastination

He Waited Too Long!

One winter day the body of a dead animal was seen floating down the Niagara River upon a cake of ice. An eagle, soaring above the river, spied it and dropped down upon it. He sat there leisurely devouring his easy prey. The swift current began bearing him rapidly downward to the falls. But was he not safe? Could he not leap in a moment into midair from his dangerous post? Could he not stretch his great pinions and float off into safety at the very brink of the awful cataract? Had he not done that a thousand times before in his bird experience? So he floated on.

But by and by came the thundering roar of the great cataract. The cloud of white mist that marked the fatal brink of the falls was towering above him. It was time to leave. So he stretched out his great wings for flight. But he could not rise! It was not that he had eaten too much and was too heavy, but, unnoted by him, his talons, sunken in the ice, and the flesh of his prey, had frozen hard and fast in the bitter winter day, and his fate was sealed! He flapped his great wings. He struggled with all the power of muscle and sinew. But all in vain. In a few moments he was swept over the abyss to his death. *He had waited too long!*

Scripture says, "Besides this you know what hour it is, how it is full time now for you to wake from sleep. For salvation is nearer to us now than when we first believed" (Rom. 13:11). There are those who have been exposed to the good news of salvation in Jesus Christ, who act as though they can procrastinate, can put off, can decide just when full commitment will be made to Almighty God. Placing feet firmly upon the transcient "facts" of life, the worldly wise feel there is no hurry. Remembering the times past when "close calls" were experienced and how it was possible by some unusual incident to defy apparent death, the same individual believes he can toy around with his eternal destiny.

Gradualism, that word that is the bane of the socially conscious person as well as the struggling minorities, has seemingly become more and more popular with so many in the realm of the spiritual. It appears that the thinking of twentieth-century man is "Let's forget about those things that pertain to the divine and think only of those things that satisfy the human ego and senses." Placing "talons" on the "ice flow" of superficial life one unknowingly becomes truly a prisoner. Too often the tragedy of life is that when escape is attempted total life is "frozen" solid in that "flow" that leads to destruction. "He waited too long!"

Procrastination

"Lie By Till Morning"

The steamship *Central America,* on a voyage from New York to San Francisco, sprang a leak in mid-ocean. Another vessel, seeing the signal of distress coming from the ship, bore down toward her. Perceiving the danger to be immediate and pressing, the captain of the rescue ship spoke to the *Central America,* asking, "What is amiss?" "We are in bad repair, and going down. Lie by till morning!" "Let me take your passengers on board *now,*" said the would-be rescuer. It was night, and the captain of the *Central America* did not like to transfer his passengers then, lest some might be lost in the confusion and the darkness, and thinking that they would keep afloat some hours longer, replied, "Lie by till morning!" Once again the captain of the rescue ship called: "You had better let me take them now." "Lie by till morning," was sounded back through the night. About an hour and a half later, the lights of the ship that was in difficulty were missed! The *Central America* had gone down, and all on board perished, because it was thought they would be saved at a later time.

How many people are there who continue to procrastinate concerning their relationship with the living Christ, the Savior? Youth, with its strength and vitality, cannot be bothered by the "confining message of God." "Later on, when there is more time, I'll consider the spiritual part of my life," cries the strong one. "I will have more time—tomorrow," says the busy person of this world. In other words, "Lie by till morning!" The Romans, of the time of Paul, were admonished by that great man of God, "Besides, this you know what hour it is, how it is full time now for you to wake from sleep. For salvation is nearer to us now than when we first believed; the night is far gone, the day is at hand" (Rom. 13:11-12a). In other words the message of a loving God is, "Let me take your passengers on board *now!"*

No thinking person questions the uncertainty of life. No one, hearing and reading the events of this present time, doubts for a moment that one nervous finger can push a button that will destroy civilization. There is not a single person alive who dares look confidently into an unknown future. Our "ships" are in bad repair. Dare we wait until "morning"?

Procrastination

Tomorrow May Be Too Late

A man once had a vision in which he seemed to be standing in the midst of an assembly of evil spirits. On the throne sat their dark ruler Satan grasping the scepter of wickedness in his hand. Summoning his subjects about him, Satan said in a loud voice, "Who will go to earth and persuade men to accomplish the ruin of their souls?"

One of the attendant spirits said, "I will go." "And how will you persuade them?" asked the grim monarch. "I will persuade them," was the answer, "that there is no heaven." But Satan replied: "No, that will not do. You will never be able to force such a belief on the general group of mankind."

Then a second spoke up and said, "I will go." "And how will you persuade them?" asked Satan. "I will persuade them that there is no hell." But again Satan answered: "You will never persuade the general public that that is so, for conscience will witness against you. We must have something which will appeal to all classes and ages and dispositions and which will be acceptable to the human race as a whole."

Thereupon a dark spirit glided forward and said, "Satan, I will go." "And what will you tell them?" asked Satan. "I will tell them," answered the spirit, "that there is no hurry." He was the spirit chosen to go—and still he is abroad in the earth.

Many people living today, as in years past, suffer from the dread disease of procrastination—that of putting off what is needed and neccessary at the time. Fortunes have been lost, promotions have been given to others, legislation has been ignored, simply because someone thought there was no hurry. One sadly wonders how many people "hurry." Too many are like Felix who told Paul he would hear him out at "a more convenient season."

The psalmist said, "When I think of thy ways, I turn my feet to thy testimonies; I hasten and do not delay to keep thy commandments" (Ps. 119:59-60). He felt the urgency to be right with God in all his earthly activities. He did not believe "there was no hurry." Today we live in uncertainty. Can we honestly think our eternal fate and destiny can wait for us to make up our minds concerning the urgent need to honor and respect God by correct attitudes and actions toward injustices? Toward laxness in moral judgments? Toward unholy alliances of expediency in the political world? Toward true involvement in the affairs of fellow humans?

Only when we are "right" with God, in Christ, can we hope to have things "right" in the world. Tomorrow may be too late!

Procrastination

Why Take the Medicine Now?

The following article appeared in *Gospel Herald*: "An earnest Christian doctor one day called to see an old man whom he had frequently visited before. The old fellow was suffering from an attack of bronchitis. This doctor made the necessary inquiries, and after promising to get some medicine ready when called for, he was about to say 'good-by' when the patient's wife asked, 'When must

John take the medicine, sir?' 'Let me see; you are not very ill; suppose you begin to take it a month from today.' 'A month from today, sir?' they cried in astonishment. 'Yes, why not? Is that too soon?' 'Too soon! Why, sir, I may be dead then!' said the patient. 'That is true; but you must remember you really are not very bad yet. Still, perhaps you had better begin to take it in a week.' 'But, sir,' cried John in great perplexity, 'begging your pardon, but I might not live a week.' 'Of course, you may not, John, but very likely you will, and the medicine will be in the house; it will keep, and if you find yourself getting worse, you could take some. I shan't charge anything for it. If you should feel worse tomorrow even, you might begin then.' 'Sir, I thought you would tell me to begin today.' 'Begin today by all means,' said the doctor, kindly. 'I only wanted to show you how false your own reasoning is, when you put off taking the medicine which the Great Physician has provided for your sin-sick soul. Just think how long you have neglected the remedy He has provided. For years you have turned away from the Lord Jesus. You have said to yourself, 'next week,' or 'next year,' or 'when I am on my deathbed, I will seek the Lord'; any time rather than the present. And yet the present is the only time that you are sure of. God's offer is only for today. Remember, 'Now is the day of salvation.' You may be dead tomorrow!''

"Behold, now is the acceptable time; behold, now is the day of salvation" (II Cor. 6:2). The emphasis is on the *"now."* Too many people are placing in the future their idea and hope of being right with God. So often the feeling is evidenced, "Let me do my thing, in my own way, until I am near the close of life. Then I will make my peace with God." But how close is anyone to "the end"? Who knows when the moment of accounting will be? Will we wait for a year, a month, a week, or even a day? Better to take the healing medicine *now*.

Reconciliation

A Valid "Claim Check"

There is a story told of a cottage in a little country village, in which lived a family of four: father, mother, and two small children. One evening something happened, what, no one knows —and the little cottage caught on fire. In a few seconds the thatched roof and wooden timbers were ablaze. There was no fire engine in this remote spot, and the villagers stood around help-lessly. But suddenly a young man, who had only recently come to the place, came striding up. "What! can nothing be done to rescue the people in there?" he cried, and as no one responded, he dashed through the flames. A moment later, he emerged bearing under each arm a little child. They were unhurt, for Andy had hidden them under his coat—but he was terribly burned. Scarcely had he gotten out before the roof fell in with a sickening crash, and the parents of the children were never seen alive again. A kind woman took Andy into her home and nursed him carefully. Meanwhile, there was much discussion in the village as to what was to become of the two rescued children. It was decided that a council should meet to decide what was to happen to them. When the day of the decision arrived, there were two who claimed the little ones. The first was the squire of the village. He had money, position, and a home to offer the children. The second claimant was—Andy! When asked what right he had to the little ones, he never said a word, but held up his hands—burned and scarred for them. It was Andy who had the valid and meaningful "claim check."

There are many people today who are living as though the Lord God has no claim upon them. They act as though they are creatures who owe loyalty and allegiance to no one else except themselves. If asked why such a philosophy is theirs they contend that there is no reason under the sun why one should bow before a person called Jesus Christ, Savior of the world. The Lord still comes, as He did to His disciples, after His resurrection and says, "See my hands and my feet. . ." (Luke 24:39a). The imprint of nails on hands and feet are His "claim check" upon every person. It was God's Son, the Savior and Redeemer who came into this world to salvage us from the burning ravages of sin. No one else was capable of performing this act of reconciliation with Almighty God. Can anyone show a more "valid claim check"?

Responsibility

"The Name's the Same"

The story is told of a soldier in the army of Alexander the Great, who was brought before the great world-conqueror for court-martial. When the emperor had listened to the charges and the evidence, he turned to the soldier facing condemnation, and said, "What is your name?" After being questioned the second time the soldier answered, "Alexander!" With a cry of rage, the emperor roared, "I say, what is your name?" And when the soldier answered for the third time, "Alexander!" the great general replied, "You say your name is Alexander? You are found guilty of your crime as charged, and now you must pay the penalty. Either change your conduct or change your name, for no man can bear the name of Alexander, my name, and do the things that you have done."

There seems to be a moral in this story. Many people bear the title "Christian"—"a Christ-man"—and yet by word and deed they belie in everyday living the position they pretend. Whereas the Christ was a man of love and concern, His followers often fail to practice the same qualities. Whereas the Christ lived and died sacrificially, those who should proudly bear the title "Christian" live self-centeredly. Whereas the Christ remained true to His convictions, His followers fluctuate and vacillate, not only in actions, but in words. The desire to willingly suffer, if necessary, for the sake of the Savior, is considered too dangerous and too confining to the pleasures of life.

In his First Letter Peter writes in part, ". . . if one suffers as a Christian, let him not be ashamed, but under that name let him glorify God" (4:16). There are so many areas in life that need the cleansing and purifying love of God. Those who are called "Christ-men" should feel the pride of the name and do nothing to jeopardize the reputation of Him who bore it gladly and willingly while He lived on this earth. As the unworthy soldier by the name of Alexander was told to either "change your conduct or change your name," so also is the Christian reminded to "walk in the spirit."

The name's the same—"Christians." Let him who would hold the torch high that has emblazoned on it the code, conduct, and creed of Jesus, the Christ, remember the high and holy task that he has—a task that carries with it highest honor and glory—and proudly act the part of a co-worker in God's kingdom seeking to win lives for all eternity. "Now then we are ambassadors for Christ . . ." (II Cor. 5:20 KJV); "We then, as workers together with him . . ." (II Cor. 6:1 KJV).

Giving Is Living

It seems that it happened this way, one time, years ago, in New Zealand. Two men met together, one for the purpose of asking the other to make a pledge to the church, the other to answer the request. The man asked to make a pledge said, "It seems to me all the church ever does is ask for money. Money, money, money, that's all they want." The man seeking the pledge answered him and said, "When my son was a little boy, he was costly; he always wanted boots and shoes, stockings and clothes, and wore them out faster than I was seemingly able to provide. The older he grew the more money had to be spent on him. But now he hasn't cost me a penny for more than a year." "How's that?" inquired the first. "Well, he died," replied the second.

Yes, the church is always asking for money. Money that can be used to alleviate the suffering, the distress, the ignorance of the world. Money is needed to continue to proclaim to a sinful world the glorious message of deliverance from the frustrations of this world through the wonderful acts of a divine Savior. It is incumbent upon those who believe the life we now live has meaning only when it is related to the heavenly purpose of God, in Christ, to support the efforts she holds dear. Saint Paul, the world's greatest missionary, once said, "Each one must do as he has made up his mind, not reluctantly or under compulsion, for God loves a cheerful giver" (II Cor. 9:7). When an individual, or a group of individuals, representing the purpose of God, no longer is willing to support the effort, he or the group will find there is no cost to Kingdom membership, but will also find out that "he died."

There is a cost in being a disciple of the Lord. Living in a world of activity and cost, the church finds itself battling against tremendous odds. Confronted by demands that all the social organizations make upon its members, the church discovers its mission is failing because of needed funds. It is fine to talk about the "spirit" of the group, but it takes more than "spirit." One depends upon divine guidance, but one also realizes that "money must be placed where the mouth is." Support of the goals of the kingdom of God is an act of worship in itself. If one wants to live within the Kingdom, one must be willing to give, for "Giving is living." This giving means of self and of one's possessions for the Lord's sake.

More Than Traditional Giving

Many years ago, in the reign of Queen Victoria the Good, the Punjab came under the British crown. The young maharajah, then a mere boy, sent as an offering to his new monarch the wonderful Koh-i-noor diamond, and it was placed, together with the other crown jewels, in the Tower of London. Several years later, the maharajah, now a full-grown man, came to England and visited Buckingham Palace, asking to see the queen. He was shown to the state apartments, and after making his formal statement of undying loyalty to Her Majesty, he asked to see the fabulous, priceless Koh-i-noor diamond. Greatly wondering at his request, the queen with her usual kindness and courtesy, gave orders that the jewel should be sent for, and that it should be brought under armed guard from the Tower to Buckingham Palace. In due time it arrived and was carried to the state apartments, and handed to the maharajah, while all present watched eagerly to see what he would do. Taking the priceless jewel with great reverence in his hand, he walked back with it clasped in his hand, and knelt at the feet of the queen. "Your Highness," he said, greatly moved, "I gave you this jewel when I was a child, too young to know what I was doing. I want to give it again, in the fullness of my strength, with all my heart, and affection, and gratitude, now and forever, fully realizing all that I do."

There is a moral, or a lesson of some sort, in that story. How often isn't it the case that one has given, in an unthinking way, the promise to be faithful to the many principles of the Christian faith? Perhaps as a child, as a matter of routine, one "gave" himself to the study of the Word, professed a belief in it, and was "received" into the so-called Fellowship of the Concerned. This was done because mom or dad, or a sainted grandmother, took one to Sunday school. It was too early in life to have any other meaning than "this is what is expected of us according to our way of life." It is necessary to rethink the meaning of giving one's self to God intellectually as well as emotionally. Paul says (II Cor. 9:7), "Each one must do as he has made up his mind, not reluctantly or under compulsion, for God loves a *cheerful* giver." Lip service is not enough for the Christian. Habits can be good, but even a good habit can lose its force if the meaning is forgotten. We must understand the need for a continuous and thoughtful giving to the Source of all gifts. Let us make our response to God more than traditional giving.

"I Hope You Will Be There"

In a book entitled *Children's Letters to God,* compiled by Eric Marshall and Stuart Hampie, there is this one: "Dear God, We are going on vacation for 2 weeks Friday. So we won't be in church. I hope you will be there when we get back. When do you take your Vacation?"

This perhaps brings a smile to our faces as we read the thoughts of a naive little child. But underneath this apparent whimsical and simple statement lies a profound thought, and maybe even an indictment. "I hope you will be there when we get back." Is it possible for a church to become so encased in religious finery, ceremony, and symbolic "trappings" that the God whose person and principles it is supposed to espouse and reveal is actually hidden? Can it be that there is a real danger of losing Him "from whom all blessings flow" in superficiality and ritual?

The ever-present God has said, "I will never fail you nor forsake you" (Heb. 13:5). This divine assurance goes beyond even the little tot's wonderment of finding Him after returning from vacation. No matter where an individual travels he can be confident the Lord God is willing and desires to watch over him, guide him, and protect him. There is nowhere one can go where one must be concerned whether God will be his complete guardian. Anyone who knows the true heart of God never needs to fear. God is always "there" wherever "there" may be. Love so encompassing defies human understanding.

Today's society finds itself caught up in a maelstrom of sinister words that seemingly advocate violence, upheaval, destruction, and annihilation of the races. "Power," "Nationalism," and "Militancy" are a few of them. Man seems determined to bring to an end all that God desires him to hold dear. And all this evil upheaval comes in the name of "gaining basic rights," of "protecting basic rights." One wonders what would happen if all people (and this includes *every* person) would appeal to the wishes and rights of the God of creation.

Whether it is over a mediation table between Labor and Management or whether over a mediation table between races cannot the highest and noblest of God's creation call upon divine guidance and justice to prevail? Figuratively, could we not take a "vacation for two weeks Friday" and pray to God saying, "I hope You will be there when we get back"?

Victory in Christ

Wellington Defeated

Apr 1986

Winchester, England is famous for its college and its cathedral. In fact, the song "Winchester Cathedral" was quite popular several years ago. A number of years before that, longer than one would want to remember, as the saying goes, the virger (the one responsible for the interior care of the church) used to tell the story of the momentary shock and dismay that came over the people of England, due to a misunderstanding. The Battle of Waterloo was being fought and all the people were vitally interested in its outcome. If Napoleon's forces defeated the Duke of Wellington there would be the dismal future of living under the emperor of France. Since there was no such thing as telegraphy in those days a sailship was to semaphore the news to a signalman on top of Winchester Cathedral. He, in turn, signaled to another man on a hill and thus the news of the battle was to be relayed, by hand semaphore, from station to station to London and all across England. When the ship came, the signalman on board semaphored the first word—"Wellington." The next was "defeated," and then the fog came down and the ship could not be seen. "Wellington defeated" went across England, and there was great gloom over the countryside. After about two or three hours, the fog lifted, and the signal came again: "Wellington defeated the enemy." Then came great rejoicing.

There was a day twenty centuries ago when gloom filled the world. The word spread—"and [they] laid him in a tomb which had been hewn out of the rock; and he rolled a stone against the door of the tomb" (Mark 15:46). As far as the critics and enemies of Jesus Christ were concerned the message was "Jesus defeated." All the principles of right and fairness and hope were laid quietly to rest. Injustice had prevailed. Man, in his self-centeredness, was in control of the universe. Evil was king! The spirit of love was laid aside once and for all. Men were now saying, "Everything is ended, all is gone, sin has conquered, man is defeated, wrong has triumphed." But the "fog" lifted three days later. Jesus Christ rose from the dead! The grave did not contain Him! Truth not only survived but in its rising, in the person of the resurrected Lord and Savior, still holds high the banner of hope.

The short-sightedness of materialistic men is beclouded with the "fog" of greed and avarice. In divine economy God perpetuated the assurance of victory. For the Christian it is not "Jesus defeated" but "Jesus defeated the evil of Satan and godless man!"

Witnessing

Can You Identify Yourself?

Adelina Patti, the great singer of past years, instructed her home post office to forward her mail to a post office in a small French village. There she planned to pick it up. "Any mail for Adelina Patti?" she inquired of the postmaster to whom she was a stranger. "Yes," replied the postmaster, "but you have to identify yourself." She presented a visiting card which the postmaster said was insufficient evidence. "What can I do?" wondered the singer. Then a brilliant idea came to her. She began to sing. In a few moments the post office was filled with people listening in wonderment to the rapturous voice. As she concluded her song, she asked the postmaster, "Are you satisfied now that I am Adelina Patti?" "Abundantly satisfied," he said apologetically. "Only Adelina Patti could sing as you have sung," and with no hesitation he gave her a bundle of mail.

The question must often be raised by those who stand "outside" the church of Jesus Christ: "Can you prove you are a Christian and that you believe all that your Leader taught?" In other words, the world still asks each person who professes faith in the God-Man, Jesus, the Lord Christ, to show an "identification tag." "Prove it!" they say.

The apostle Paul knew the need for example and "identification." He wrote to his Philippian friends, "Finally, brethren, whatever is true, whatever is honorable, whatever is just, whatever is pure, whatever is lovely, whatever is gracious, if there is any excellence, if there is anything worthy of praise, think about these things. What you have learned and received and heard and seen in me, do; and the God of peace will be with you" (4:8-9).

There is a way by which one can be known as a Christian. Even as the great Adelina Patti was identified by the sound of her voice, so the Christian can be "identified" by his every action and deed. Someone has said that the very devil himself is willing for a person to confess Christianity so long as he does not practice it. There are numerous avenues open to the Christian to "identify" with Christ. He cannot remain silent in the face of injustice, hate, greed, violence, war, and selfish concerns if he is truly a Christ-follower. He will speak out, act in defense of the downtrodden, and reveal a deep and concerned love for justice, peace, and harmony. Does the way you live identify you as one of God's children?

Witnessing

The Connecting Link

25 Sep 83

When King George V of England was about to make a radio address supporting the disarmanent program, after the First World War, it was discovered a few minutes before the program began that a wire leading to the microphone was broken and that there was not sufficent time to make repairs. The young radio technician who made the discovery grasped the two ends of the wire and became the current link, and the king's voice, passing through his body, was heard around the world.

"A connecting link, . . . heard around the world!" What an apt description of the truly activated Christian. At a time when there is such a tremendous need for the spreading of the good news of the everlasting love of God toward man, certainly each one who professes a belief in divine mercy, through Jesus Christ, will want to be that link through which passes the voice of God. The Lord has promised that we can be "clothed with power from on high" (Luke 24:49). That power which is available for the Christian is the strength of the Spirit that will lead in proper paths and give insight into the situations that confront us.

If there is any indictment to be made in our age it cannot be made against the principles Christ's church is to proclaim. The unshakeable truths embodied in the life of Him who came to earth to bring to man redemption and the assurance of eternal life are still the same. The indictment falls on those who wish to be considered members of the body of the Savior but who fail to make their profession become active and alive. There is a responsibility that every child of God carries within himself. That responsibility is to show, by acts of love, the "aliveness" of God and His everlasting searching for the hearts and lives of the whole of humanity. God looks to sanctified sinners to keep "the circuit" open and alive.

"Time is of the essence" has become almost a trite statement; however, it is no less true now than when it was first spoken. Man has attempted to find relief from sorrows, hurt, and frustrating disappointments. Humanistic philosophies have been tried. Pleasure for pleasure's sake has proved a failure. Eroticism, in all forms, has left a void. There is only one hope for humanity—the way of God in Christ! Each Christian must serve as "the connecting link."

Witnessing

Indirect Advertising Sells

A number of years ago, near what is known as the Kingsport Press in Tennessee, a southbound bus made scheduled midday stops of twenty minutes so that passengers might freshen up and get a bit to eat. One driver said, as he brought his bus to a stop: "Folks, we'll be stopping here for twenty minutes. This line makes it a strict policy never to recommend an eating place by name, but if anybody wants me while we're here, I'll be eating a wonderful T-bone steak with french fries at Tony's first-class, spotlessly clean diner directly across the street." With that remark he slowly sauntered into the tiny but tidy restaurant. Naturally, a number of the passengers on the bus took his advice and went into the eating establishment. It came as no surprise to them that the meals they ordered were very good. The bus driver had done a good job in his "soft sell" through indirect appeal.

It would seem that many more people could be attracted to the Christian faith if those who make a profession of faith would invite by "indirection," by living lives that show clearly that their faith is more than mere "mouthings of pious phrases."

The Man of Nazareth, Jesus Christ, has said, ". . . you shall be my witnesses . . ." (Acts 1:8). It is the believer who reveals Christ by the way he lives, moves, walks, talks, eats, reads, pays his bills, keeps his home in pleasant condition, is concerned with his neighbor's welfare, fights injustice, leads in action for better human relations, stands for social equality, and a thousand other details in life. He undoubtedly does much more than the fanatic with the sandwich board that reads, "Prepare to meet thy God," or who stands on a street corner trying to "buttonhole" passers-by with the phrase, "Are you saved?" The "indirect sell" and the "soft sell" make the principles of Jesus Christ meaningful and applicable to life as it is lived everyday.

There is nothing to stop the follower of Christ recommending Him as the only Source and Hope for meaningful life. The Savior does not forbid any of His own to speak out for Him and the new relationship with God bought with His own blood. However, if the Christian desires to serve and love His Lord he must seek out areas of service to his brother man. "Inasmuch as you have done it unto one of the least of these my brethren, you have done it unto me," says our Lord. Indirect advertising sells the kingdom of God! Try it!

Witnessing

It's Written on Your Face

Leonardo da Vinci was one of Italy's greatest artists. In addition, he was a poet, sculptor, architect, philosopher, musician, scientist, and machinist. He wasn't just a "dabbler"; instead he was a master in all that he did. The most outstanding work of art he performed was "The Last Supper" that was painted on the wall of a convent. A story has come down through the years about it that may or may not be true. It does, however, give rise to serious reflection. It seems the artist wanted to paint the central figure first and that figure was Christ. He searched for some young man to model for the picture. In the choir of the church in Milan was a handsome man with mild and gentle features and with a personality marked with intelligence and culture. It appeared he was everything the sincere Christian should be. For months Pedro Bandandello, the model, stood before the artist in the pose desired, until the figure of Christ was completed. Years passed by as da Vinci painted all the other figures except Judas, the treacherous hypocrite and thief. Again the search for one whose facial expressions portrayed a life of sin and dissipation began. Finally a man was found in an out-of-the-way tavern noted for its degradation. Offered money to pose for the Judas face, the man accepted. Months passed before the final features of the betraying Judas were placed on the picture. To the amazement of the artist, he discovered that Peter Bandandello was the same man who had posed for the portrait of the Christ. Eight years had passed from the first posing to the last, and in those years Pedro's appearance had so changed that he fitted the description of the Betrayer.

"Be sure your sin will find you out" (Num. 32:23) we are told. The "face of Christ" can only be seen in the individual who walks with Him along all of life's paths. Too often people feel they can pursue the fleeting interests of a sinful world without its having any effect upon them. There is a beauty that is much more than "skin-deep" about those who have surrendered themselves to the way of heavenly love. The beauty of concern for one's fellowman as well as the beauty of involvement in the cause of eternity will show clearly. It will be written on your face.

Witnessing

The Light Shines Through

A little boy was accustomed to attending a church that had beautiful stained-glass windows in the sanctuary. He was familiar with the Good Shepherd window as well as others that portrayed various events in the earthly life of Jesus Christ. Also in the church were windows with the figures of Saint Matthew, Saint Mark, Saint Luke, Saint John, and Saint Paul. These beautiful windows were a source of curiosity as well as impressiveness to the boy. One day as he was standing looking at them an older member of the congregation approached him and pointing to one of the "saint" windows asked, "What is a saint?" For a moment the boy seemed stumped for an answer, then brightening up answered, "A saint is a person the light shines through."

In the Gospel of Matthew we read the words of the Savior, as He spoke to His followers: "Let your light so shine before men, that they may see your good works and give glory to your Father who is in heaven" (5:16). A Christian is to be "seen" by his good works! This is an imperative statement. There is no question in the mind of our Lord when He gives the direct admonition to those who would bear the title "Christian." There is no such thing as being a "passive Christian" when we think of the need to fill the community with words and deeds that reflect heavenly love.

Often the "churchman" wonders what he can do. Often the feeling is expressed that one does not have the ability to "sell" the Christian faith. No matter how little formal education one has or how obscure an individual may be in comparison to the "name" person, he has unlimited opportunity to show his Christian faith by attitudes and actions that reflect the concern his Master had toward the total man.

If the "light"—the Light of the World—does not shine through one's own living there must be serious doubts about his faith. Either it is an unmeaning mouthing of the "Profession of Faith" or it is based on some false and human reasoning. In either case it falls far short of the expectation of Him who desired that "they [the world] may see your good works and give glory to God who is in heaven." Always alert, the man of God will place himself in the position of doing "good"—activating himself to the cause of man's spiritual and bodily hope. There is a requirement placed upon faith. One cannot hide in the darkness of silence. The Christian must allow the light to shine through.

Witnessing

Tell It When You Can

Dr. R. A. Torrey tells of an incident in his life while he was eating dinner with a friend, a Mr. Alexander, in a restaurant, in Brighton, England. While in the course of the dinner, one of the people on the evangelistic staff noticed that the waiter appeared to be much troubled. Into his heart and mind came the overpowering thought that he should speak to the man and try to bring to him some comfort, in the name of God. Each time he was about to speak with the waiter something took place. Besides the conflicting activities, the missionary felt that it was a most unusual thing to do, and the situation would cause embarrassment both to himself and to the waiter. The meal ended and the bill was paid. The concerned man stepped out of the restaurant, but still retained the feeling that he should talk to the waiter in question.

He waited outside the restaurant for the man to come out after his tasks were finished. It was only a short time later when the owner of the establishment came through the door, turned the key in the lock, and started for home. Noticing the man who had recently eaten in his place of business, he went to him and asked why he was standing nearby and whether he could help him in any way. The evangelistic missionary said he was waiting for the man who had served him. The proprietor replied, "You will never speak to him again. After waiting on you he went to his room, locked the door, took a pistol from the dresser drawer, and shot himself dead!" Saddened and with a feeling of self-incrimination, the missionary realized he had lost eternally the opportunity to bring a word of encouragement and meaning to life to one who was so much in need of knowing there was a "Someone" who cared for him.

The young man, Timothy, follower of Christ, through Paul, was admonished by his spiritual father to "preach the word, be urgent in season . . ." (II Tim. 4:2). There are so many times the Christian has opportunity to speak quietly, and with conviction, about the grace of God in his own life but *fails to do so!* Either one is embarrassed or too busy. Or one feels that another time might be more appropriate. But each of us has only today, so we should tell the glorious message of salvation, in Christ, *when we can!*